C-1764   CAREER EXAMINATION SERIES

This is your
PASSBOOK for...

Principal Planner

Test Preparation Study Guide
Questions & Answers

COPYRIGHT NOTICE

This book is SOLELY intended for, is sold ONLY to, and its use is RESTRICTED to individual, bona fide applicants or candidates who qualify by virtue of having seriously filed applications for appropriate license, certificate, professional and/or promotional advancement, higher school matriculation, scholarship, or other legitimate requirements of education and/or governmental authorities.

This book is NOT intended for use, class instruction, tutoring, training, duplication, copying, reprinting, excerption, or adaptation, etc., by:

1) Other publishers
2) Proprietors and/or Instructors of "Coaching" and/or Preparatory Courses
3) Personnel and/or Training Divisions of commercial, industrial, and governmental organizations
4) Schools, colleges, or universities and/or their departments and staffs, including teachers and other personnel
5) Testing Agencies or Bureaus
6) Study groups which seek by the purchase of a single volume to copy and/or duplicate and/or adapt this material for use by the group as a whole without having purchased individual volumes for each of the members of the group
7) Et al.

Such persons would be in violation of appropriate Federal and State statutes.

PROVISION OF LICENSING AGREEMENTS – Recognized educational, commercial, industrial, and governmental institutions and organizations, and others legitimately engaged in educational pursuits, including training, testing, and measurement activities, may address request for a licensing agreement to the copyright owners, who will determine whether, and under what conditions, including fees and charges, the materials in this book may be used them. In other words, a licensing facility exists for the legitimate use of the material in this book on other than an individual basis. However, it is asseverated and affirmed here that the material in this book CANNOT be used without the receipt of the express permission of such a licensing agreement from the Publishers. Inquiries re licensing should be addressed to the company, attention rights and permissions department.

All rights reserved, including the right of reproduction in whole or in part, in any form or by any means, electronic or mechanical, including photocopying, recording, or by any information storage and retrieval system, without permission in writing from the Publisher.

Copyright © 2025 by
National Learning Corporation

212 Michael Drive, Syosset, NY 11791
(516) 921-8888 • www.passbooks.com
E-mail: info@passbooks.com

PASSBOOK® SERIES

THE *PASSBOOK® SERIES* has been created to prepare applicants and candidates for the ultimate academic battlefield – the examination room.

At some time in our lives, each and every one of us may be required to take an examination – for validation, matriculation, admission, qualification, registration, certification, or licensure.

Based on the assumption that every applicant or candidate has met the basic formal educational standards, has taken the required number of courses, and read the necessary texts, the *PASSBOOK® SERIES* furnishes the one special preparation which may assure passing with confidence, instead of failing with insecurity. Examination questions – together with answers – are furnished as the basic vehicle for study so that the mysteries of the examination and its compounding difficulties may be eliminated or diminished by a sure method.

This book is meant to help you pass your examination provided that you qualify and are serious in your objective.

The entire field is reviewed through the huge store of content information which is succinctly presented through a provocative and challenging approach – the question-and-answer method.

A climate of success is established by furnishing the correct answers at the end of each test.

You soon learn to recognize types of questions, forms of questions, and patterns of questioning. You may even begin to anticipate expected outcomes.

You perceive that many questions are repeated or adapted so that you can gain acute insights, which may enable you to score many sure points.

You learn how to confront new questions, or types of questions, and to attack them confidently and work out the correct answers.

You note objectives and emphases, and recognize pitfalls and dangers, so that you may make positive educational adjustments.

Moreover, you are kept fully informed in relation to new concepts, methods, practices, and directions in the field.

You discover that you are actually taking the examination all the time: you are preparing for the examination by "taking" an examination, not by reading extraneous and/or supererogatory textbooks.

In short, this PASSBOOK®, used directedly, should be an important factor in helping you to pass your test.

PRINCIPAL PLANNER

DUTIES:
An employee in this class coordinates and develops programs and plans for a particular department or agency. The incumbent supervises and reviews the work of clerical, technical and professional personnel in various planning studies. Supervision is received from an administrative supervisor through conferences and written reports. Does related work as required.

SCOPE OF THE EXAMINATION:
The written test will cover knowledge, skills, and/or abilities in such areas as:
1. Administrative supervision;
2. Collection, analysis, and presentation of data;
3. Principles and practices of project management;
4. Community and regional physical planning, including zoning and subdivision regulations;
5. Principles and practices of urban planning;
6. Community development program planning, including related federal and state laws and programs;
7. Preparing written material.

HOW TO TAKE A TEST

I. YOU MUST PASS AN EXAMINATION

A. *WHAT EVERY CANDIDATE SHOULD KNOW*

Examination applicants often ask us for help in preparing for the written test. What can I study in advance? What kinds of questions will be asked? How will the test be given? How will the papers be graded?

As an applicant for a civil service examination, you may be wondering about some of these things. Our purpose here is to suggest effective methods of advance study and to describe civil service examinations.

Your chances for success on this examination can be increased if you know how to prepare. Those "pre-examination jitters" can be reduced if you know what to expect. You can even experience an adventure in good citizenship if you know why civil service exams are given.

B. *WHY ARE CIVIL SERVICE EXAMINATIONS GIVEN?*

Civil service examinations are important to you in two ways. As a citizen, you want public jobs filled by employees who know how to do their work. As a job seeker, you want a fair chance to compete for that job on an equal footing with other candidates. The best-known means of accomplishing this two-fold goal is the competitive examination.

Exams are widely publicized throughout the nation. They may be administered for jobs in federal, state, city, municipal, town or village governments or agencies.

Any citizen may apply, with some limitations, such as the age or residence of applicants. Your experience and education may be reviewed to see whether you meet the requirements for the particular examination. When these requirements exist, they are reasonable and applied consistently to all applicants. Thus, a competitive examination may cause you some uneasiness now, but it is your privilege and safeguard.

C. *HOW ARE CIVIL SERVICE EXAMS DEVELOPED?*

Examinations are carefully written by trained technicians who are specialists in the field known as "psychological measurement," in consultation with recognized authorities in the field of work that the test will cover. These experts recommend the subject matter areas or skills to be tested; only those knowledges or skills important to your success on the job are included. The most reliable books and source materials available are used as references. Together, the experts and technicians judge the difficulty level of the questions.

Test technicians know how to phrase questions so that the problem is clearly stated. Their ethics do not permit "trick" or "catch" questions. Questions may have been tried out on sample groups, or subjected to statistical analysis, to determine their usefulness.

Written tests are often used in combination with performance tests, ratings of training and experience, and oral interviews. All of these measures combine to form the best-known means of finding the right person for the right job.

II. HOW TO PASS THE WRITTEN TEST

A. NATURE OF THE EXAMINATION

To prepare intelligently for civil service examinations, you should know how they differ from school examinations you have taken. In school you were assigned certain definite pages to read or subjects to cover. The examination questions were quite detailed and usually emphasized memory. Civil service exams, on the other hand, try to discover your present ability to perform the duties of a position, plus your potentiality to learn these duties. In other words, a civil service exam attempts to predict how successful you will be. Questions cover such a broad area that they cannot be as minute and detailed as school exam questions.

In the public service similar kinds of work, or positions, are grouped together in one "class." This process is known as *position-classification*. All the positions in a class are paid according to the salary range for that class. One class title covers all of these positions, and they are all tested by the same examination.

B. FOUR BASIC STEPS

1) Study the announcement

How, then, can you know what subjects to study? Our best answer is: "Learn as much as possible about the class of positions for which you've applied." The exam will test the knowledge, skills and abilities needed to do the work.

Your most valuable source of information about the position you want is the official exam announcement. This announcement lists the training and experience qualifications. Check these standards and apply only if you come reasonably close to meeting them.

The brief description of the position in the examination announcement offers some clues to the subjects which will be tested. Think about the job itself. Review the duties in your mind. Can you perform them, or are there some in which you are rusty? Fill in the blank spots in your preparation.

Many jurisdictions preview the written test in the exam announcement by including a section called "Knowledge and Abilities Required," "Scope of the Examination," or some similar heading. Here you will find out specifically what fields will be tested.

2) Review your own background

Once you learn in general what the position is all about, and what you need to know to do the work, ask yourself which subjects you already know fairly well and which need improvement. You may wonder whether to concentrate on improving your strong areas or on building some background in your fields of weakness. When the announcement has specified "some knowledge" or "considerable knowledge," or has used adjectives like "beginning principles of..." or "advanced ... methods," you can get a clue as to the number and difficulty of questions to be asked in any given field. More questions, and hence broader coverage, would be included for those subjects which are more important in the work. Now weigh your strengths and weaknesses against the job requirements and prepare accordingly.

3) Determine the level of the position

Another way to tell how intensively you should prepare is to understand the level of the job for which you are applying. Is it the entering level? In other words, is this the position in which beginners in a field of work are hired? Or is it an intermediate or advanced level? Sometimes this is indicated by such words as "Junior" or "Senior" in the class title. Other jurisdictions use Roman numerals to designate the level – Clerk I, Clerk II, for example. The word "Supervisor" sometimes appears in the title. If the level is not indicated by the title, check the description of duties. Will you be working under very close supervision, or will you have responsibility for independent decisions in this work?

4) Choose appropriate study materials

Now that you know the subjects to be examined and the relative amount of each subject to be covered, you can choose suitable study materials. For beginning level jobs, or even advanced ones, if you have a pronounced weakness in some aspect of your training, read a modern, standard textbook in that field. Be sure it is up to date and has general coverage. Such books are normally available at your library, and the librarian will be glad to help you locate one. For entry-level positions, questions of appropriate difficulty are chosen – neither highly advanced questions, nor those too simple. Such questions require careful thought but not advanced training.

If the position for which you are applying is technical or advanced, you will read more advanced, specialized material. If you are already familiar with the basic principles of your field, elementary textbooks would waste your time. Concentrate on advanced textbooks and technical periodicals. Think through the concepts and review difficult problems in your field.

These are all general sources. You can get more ideas on your own initiative, following these leads. For example, training manuals and publications of the government agency which employs workers in your field can be useful, particularly for technical and professional positions. A letter or visit to the government department involved may result in more specific study suggestions, and certainly will provide you with a more definite idea of the exact nature of the position you are seeking.

III. KINDS OF TESTS

Tests are used for purposes other than measuring knowledge and ability to perform specified duties. For some positions, it is equally important to test ability to make adjustments to new situations or to profit from training. In others, basic mental abilities not dependent on information are essential. Questions which test these things may not appear as pertinent to the duties of the position as those which test for knowledge and information. Yet they are often highly important parts of a fair examination. For very general questions, it is almost impossible to help you direct your study efforts. What we can do is to point out some of the more common of these general abilities needed in public service positions and describe some typical questions.

1) General information

Broad, general information has been found useful for predicting job success in some kinds of work. This is tested in a variety of ways, from vocabulary lists to questions about current events. Basic background in some field of work, such as sociology or economics, may be sampled in a group of questions. Often these are principles which have become familiar to most persons through exposure rather than through formal training. It is difficult to advise you how to study for these questions; being alert to the world around you is our best suggestion.

2) Verbal ability

An example of an ability needed in many positions is verbal or language ability. Verbal ability is, in brief, the ability to use and understand words. Vocabulary and grammar tests are typical measures of this ability. Reading comprehension or paragraph interpretation questions are common in many kinds of civil service tests. You are given a paragraph of written material and asked to find its central meaning.

3) Numerical ability

Number skills can be tested by the familiar arithmetic problem, by checking paired lists of numbers to see which are alike and which are different, or by interpreting charts and graphs. In the latter test, a graph may be printed in the test booklet which you are asked to use as the basis for answering questions.

4) Observation

A popular test for law-enforcement positions is the observation test. A picture is shown to you for several minutes, then taken away. Questions about the picture test your ability to observe both details and larger elements.

5) Following directions

In many positions in the public service, the employee must be able to carry out written instructions dependably and accurately. You may be given a chart with several columns, each column listing a variety of information. The questions require you to carry out directions involving the information given in the chart.

6) Skills and aptitudes

Performance tests effectively measure some manual skills and aptitudes. When the skill is one in which you are trained, such as typing or shorthand, you can practice. These tests are often very much like those given in business school or high school courses. For many of the other skills and aptitudes, however, no short-time preparation can be made. Skills and abilities natural to you or that you have developed throughout your lifetime are being tested.

Many of the general questions just described provide all the data needed to answer the questions and ask you to use your reasoning ability to find the answers. Your best preparation for these tests, as well as for tests of facts and ideas, is to be at your physical and mental best. You, no doubt, have your own methods of getting into an exam-taking mood and keeping "in shape." The next section lists some ideas on this subject.

IV. KINDS OF QUESTIONS

Only rarely is the "essay" question, which you answer in narrative form, used in civil service tests. Civil service tests are usually of the short-answer type. Full instructions for answering these questions will be given to you at the examination. But in case this is your first experience with short-answer questions and separate answer sheets, here is what you need to know:

1) Multiple-choice Questions

Most popular of the short-answer questions is the "multiple choice" or "best answer" question. It can be used, for example, to test for factual knowledge, ability to solve problems or judgment in meeting situations found at work.

A multiple-choice question is normally one of three types—
- It can begin with an incomplete statement followed by several possible endings. You are to find the one ending which *best* completes the statement, although some of the others may not be entirely wrong.
- It can also be a complete statement in the form of a question which is answered by choosing one of the statements listed.

- It can be in the form of a problem – again you select the best answer.

Here is an example of a multiple-choice question with a discussion which should give you some clues as to the method for choosing the right answer:

When an employee has a complaint about his assignment, the action which will *best* help him overcome his difficulty is to
    A. discuss his difficulty with his coworkers
    B. take the problem to the head of the organization
    C. take the problem to the person who gave him the assignment
    D. say nothing to anyone about his complaint

In answering this question, you should study each of the choices to find which is best. Consider choice "A" – Certainly an employee may discuss his complaint with fellow employees, but no change or improvement can result, and the complaint remains unresolved. Choice "B" is a poor choice since the head of the organization probably does not know what assignment you have been given, and taking your problem to him is known as "going over the head" of the supervisor. The supervisor, or person who made the assignment, is the person who can clarify it or correct any injustice. Choice "C" is, therefore, correct. To say nothing, as in choice "D," is unwise. Supervisors have and interest in knowing the problems employees are facing, and the employee is seeking a solution to his problem.

2) True/False Questions

The "true/false" or "right/wrong" form of question is sometimes used. Here a complete statement is given. Your job is to decide whether the statement is right or wrong.

SAMPLE: A roaming cell-phone call to a nearby city costs less than a non-roaming call to a distant city.

This statement is wrong, or false, since roaming calls are more expensive.
This is not a complete list of all possible question forms, although most of the others are variations of these common types. You will always get complete directions for answering questions. Be sure you understand *how* to mark your answers – ask questions until you do.

V. RECORDING YOUR ANSWERS

Computer terminals are used more and more today for many different kinds of exams.
For an examination with very few applicants, you may be told to record your answers in the test booklet itself. Separate answer sheets are much more common. If this separate answer sheet is to be scored by machine – and this is often the case – it is highly important that you mark your answers correctly in order to get credit.
An electronic scoring machine is often used in civil service offices because of the speed with which papers can be scored. Machine-scored answer sheets must be marked with a pencil, which will be given to you. This pencil has a high graphite content which responds to the electronic scoring machine. As a matter of fact, stray dots may register as answers, so do not let your pencil rest on the answer sheet while you are pondering the correct answer. Also, if your pencil lead breaks or is otherwise defective, ask for another.

Since the answer sheet will be dropped in a slot in the scoring machine, be careful not to bend the corners or get the paper crumpled.

The answer sheet normally has five vertical columns of numbers, with 30 numbers to a column. These numbers correspond to the question numbers in your test booklet. After each number, going across the page are four or five pairs of dotted lines. These short dotted lines have small letters or numbers above them. The first two pairs may also have a "T" or "F" above the letters. This indicates that the first two pairs only are to be used if the questions are of the true-false type. If the questions are multiple choice, disregard the "T" and "F" and pay attention only to the small letters or numbers.

Answer your questions in the manner of the sample that follows:

32. The largest city in the United States is
    A. Washington, D.C.
    B. New York City
    C. Chicago
    D. Detroit
    E. San Francisco

1) Choose the answer you think is best. (New York City is the largest, so "B" is correct.)
2) Find the row of dotted lines numbered the same as the question you are answering. (Find row number 32)
3) Find the pair of dotted lines corresponding to the answer. (Find the pair of lines under the mark "B.")
4) Make a solid black mark between the dotted lines.

VI. BEFORE THE TEST

Common sense will help you find procedures to follow to get ready for an examination. Too many of us, however, overlook these sensible measures. Indeed, nervousness and fatigue have been found to be the most serious reasons why applicants fail to do their best on civil service tests. Here is a list of reminders:

- Begin your preparation early – Don't wait until the last minute to go scurrying around for books and materials or to find out what the position is all about.
- Prepare continuously – An hour a night for a week is better than an all-night cram session. This has been definitely established. What is more, a night a week for a month will return better dividends than crowding your study into a shorter period of time.
- Locate the place of the exam – You have been sent a notice telling you when and where to report for the examination. If the location is in a different town or otherwise unfamiliar to you, it would be well to inquire the best route and learn something about the building.
- Relax the night before the test – Allow your mind to rest. Do not study at all that night. Plan some mild recreation or diversion; then go to bed early and get a good night's sleep.
- Get up early enough to make a leisurely trip to the place for the test – This way unforeseen events, traffic snarls, unfamiliar buildings, etc. will not upset you.
- Dress comfortably – A written test is not a fashion show. You will be known by number and not by name, so wear something comfortable.

- Leave excess paraphernalia at home – Shopping bags and odd bundles will get in your way. You need bring only the items mentioned in the official notice you received; usually everything you need is provided. Do not bring reference books to the exam. They will only confuse those last minutes and be taken away from you when in the test room.
- Arrive somewhat ahead of time – If because of transportation schedules you must get there very early, bring a newspaper or magazine to take your mind off yourself while waiting.
- Locate the examination room – When you have found the proper room, you will be directed to the seat or part of the room where you will sit. Sometimes you are given a sheet of instructions to read while you are waiting. Do not fill out any forms until you are told to do so; just read them and be prepared.
- Relax and prepare to listen to the instructions
- If you have any physical problem that may keep you from doing your best, be sure to tell the test administrator. If you are sick or in poor health, you really cannot do your best on the exam. You can come back and take the test some other time.

VII. AT THE TEST

The day of the test is here and you have the test booklet in your hand. The temptation to get going is very strong. Caution! There is more to success than knowing the right answers. You must know how to identify your papers and understand variations in the type of short-answer question used in this particular examination. Follow these suggestions for maximum results from your efforts:

1) Cooperate with the monitor

The test administrator has a duty to create a situation in which you can be as much at ease as possible. He will give instructions, tell you when to begin, check to see that you are marking your answer sheet correctly, and so on. He is not there to guard you, although he will see that your competitors do not take unfair advantage. He wants to help you do your best.

2) Listen to all instructions

Don't jump the gun! Wait until you understand all directions. In most civil service tests you get more time than you need to answer the questions. So don't be in a hurry. Read each word of instructions until you clearly understand the meaning. Study the examples, listen to all announcements and follow directions. Ask questions if you do not understand what to do.

3) Identify your papers

Civil service exams are usually identified by number only. You will be assigned a number; you must not put your name on your test papers. Be sure to copy your number correctly. Since more than one exam may be given, copy your exact examination title.

4) Plan your time

Unless you are told that a test is a "speed" or "rate of work" test, speed itself is usually not important. Time enough to answer all the questions will be provided, but this does not mean that you have all day. An overall time limit has been set. Divide the total time (in minutes) by the number of questions to determine the approximate time you have for each question.

5) Do not linger over difficult questions

If you come across a difficult question, mark it with a paper clip (useful to have along) and come back to it when you have been through the booklet. One caution if you do this – be sure to skip a number on your answer sheet as well. Check often to be sure that you have not lost your place and that you are marking in the row numbered the same as the question you are answering.

6) Read the questions

Be sure you know what the question asks! Many capable people are unsuccessful because they failed to *read* the questions correctly.

7) Answer all questions

Unless you have been instructed that a penalty will be deducted for incorrect answers, it is better to guess than to omit a question.

8) Speed tests

It is often better NOT to guess on speed tests. It has been found that on timed tests people are tempted to spend the last few seconds before time is called in marking answers at random – without even reading them – in the hope of picking up a few extra points. To discourage this practice, the instructions may warn you that your score will be "corrected" for guessing. That is, a penalty will be applied. The incorrect answers will be deducted from the correct ones, or some other penalty formula will be used.

9) Review your answers

If you finish before time is called, go back to the questions you guessed or omitted to give them further thought. Review other answers if you have time.

10) Return your test materials

If you are ready to leave before others have finished or time is called, take ALL your materials to the monitor and leave quietly. Never take any test material with you. The monitor can discover whose papers are not complete, and taking a test booklet may be grounds for disqualification.

VIII. EXAMINATION TECHNIQUES

1) Read the general instructions carefully. These are usually printed on the first page of the exam booklet. As a rule, these instructions refer to the timing of the examination; the fact that you should not start work until the signal and must stop work at a signal, etc. If there are any *special* instructions, such as a choice of questions to be answered, make sure that you note this instruction carefully.

2) When you are ready to start work on the examination, that is as soon as the signal has been given, read the instructions to each question booklet, underline any key words or phrases, such as *least, best, outline, describe* and the like. In this way you will tend to answer as requested rather than discover on reviewing your paper that you *listed without describing*, that you selected the *worst* choice rather than the *best* choice, etc.

3) If the examination is of the objective or multiple-choice type – that is, each question will also give a series of possible answers: A, B, C or D, and you are called upon to select the best answer and write the letter next to that answer on your answer paper – it is advisable to start answering each question in turn. There may be anywhere from 50 to 100 such questions in the three or four hours allotted and you can see how much time would be taken if you read through all the questions before beginning to answer any. Furthermore, if you come across a question or group of questions which you know would be difficult to answer, it would undoubtedly affect your handling of all the other questions.

4) If the examination is of the essay type and contains but a few questions, it is a moot point as to whether you should read all the questions before starting to answer any one. Of course, if you are given a choice – say five out of seven and the like – then it is essential to read all the questions so you can eliminate the two that are most difficult. If, however, you are asked to answer all the questions, there may be danger in trying to answer the easiest one first because you may find that you will spend too much time on it. The best technique is to answer the first question, then proceed to the second, etc.

5) Time your answers. Before the exam begins, write down the time it started, then add the time allowed for the examination and write down the time it must be completed, then divide the time available somewhat as follows:
    - If 3-1/2 hours are allowed, that would be 210 minutes. If you have 80 objective-type questions, that would be an average of 2-1/2 minutes per question. Allow yourself no more than 2 minutes per question, or a total of 160 minutes, which will permit about 50 minutes to review.
    - If for the time allotment of 210 minutes there are 7 essay questions to answer, that would average about 30 minutes a question. Give yourself only 25 minutes per question so that you have about 35 minutes to review.

6) The most important instruction is to *read each question* and make sure you know what is wanted. The second most important instruction is to *time yourself properly* so that you answer every question. The third most important instruction is to *answer every question*. Guess if you have to but include something for each question. Remember that you will receive no credit for a blank and will probably receive some credit if you write something in answer to an essay question. If you guess a letter – say "B" for a multiple-choice question – you may have guessed right. If you leave a blank as an answer to a multiple-choice question, the examiners may respect your feelings but it will not add a point to your score. Some exams may penalize you for wrong answers, so in such cases *only*, you may not want to guess unless you have some basis for your answer.

7) Suggestions
    a. Objective-type questions
        1. Examine the question booklet for proper sequence of pages and questions
        2. Read all instructions carefully
        3. Skip any question which seems too difficult; return to it after all other questions have been answered
        4. Apportion your time properly; do not spend too much time on any single question or group of questions

5. Note and underline key words – *all, most, fewest, least, best, worst, same, opposite*, etc.
6. Pay particular attention to negatives
7. Note unusual option, e.g., unduly long, short, complex, different or similar in content to the body of the question
8. Observe the use of "hedging" words – *probably, may, most likely*, etc.
9. Make sure that your answer is put next to the same number as the question
10. Do not second-guess unless you have good reason to believe the second answer is definitely more correct
11. Cross out original answer if you decide another answer is more accurate; do not erase until you are ready to hand your paper in
12. Answer all questions; guess unless instructed otherwise
13. Leave time for review

  b. Essay questions
   1. Read each question carefully
   2. Determine exactly what is wanted. Underline key words or phrases.
   3. Decide on outline or paragraph answer
   4. Include many different points and elements unless asked to develop any one or two points or elements
   5. Show impartiality by giving pros and cons unless directed to select one side only
   6. Make and write down any assumptions you find necessary to answer the questions
   7. Watch your English, grammar, punctuation and choice of words
   8. Time your answers; don't crowd material

8) Answering the essay question

Most essay questions can be answered by framing the specific response around several key words or ideas. Here are a few such key words or ideas:

M's: manpower, materials, methods, money, management
P's: purpose, program, policy, plan, procedure, practice, problems, pitfalls, personnel, public relations
  a. Six basic steps in handling problems:
   1. Preliminary plan and background development
   2. Collect information, data and facts
   3. Analyze and interpret information, data and facts
   4. Analyze and develop solutions as well as make recommendations
   5. Prepare report and sell recommendations
   6. Install recommendations and follow up effectiveness

  b. Pitfalls to avoid
   1. *Taking things for granted* – A statement of the situation does not necessarily imply that each of the elements is necessarily true; for example, a complaint may be invalid and biased so that all that can be taken for granted is that a complaint has been registered

2. *Considering only one side of a situation* – Wherever possible, indicate several alternatives and then point out the reasons you selected the best one
3. *Failing to indicate follow up* – Whenever your answer indicates action on your part, make certain that you will take proper follow-up action to see how successful your recommendations, procedures or actions turn out to be
4. *Taking too long in answering any single question* – Remember to time your answers properly

IX. AFTER THE TEST

Scoring procedures differ in detail among civil service jurisdictions although the general principles are the same. Whether the papers are hand-scored or graded by machine we have described, they are nearly always graded by number. That is, the person who marks the paper knows only the number – never the name – of the applicant. Not until all the papers have been graded will they be matched with names. If other tests, such as training and experience or oral interview ratings have been given, scores will be combined. Different parts of the examination usually have different weights. For example, the written test might count 60 percent of the final grade, and a rating of training and experience 40 percent. In many jurisdictions, veterans will have a certain number of points added to their grades.

After the final grade has been determined, the names are placed in grade order and an eligible list is established. There are various methods for resolving ties between those who get the same final grade – probably the most common is to place first the name of the person whose application was received first. Job offers are made from the eligible list in the order the names appear on it. You will be notified of your grade and your rank as soon as all these computations have been made. This will be done as rapidly as possible.

People who are found to meet the requirements in the announcement are called "eligibles." Their names are put on a list of eligible candidates. An eligible's chances of getting a job depend on how high he stands on this list and how fast agencies are filling jobs from the list.

When a job is to be filled from a list of eligibles, the agency asks for the names of people on the list of eligibles for that job. When the civil service commission receives this request, it sends to the agency the names of the three people highest on this list. Or, if the job to be filled has specialized requirements, the office sends the agency the names of the top three persons who meet these requirements from the general list.

The appointing officer makes a choice from among the three people whose names were sent to him. If the selected person accepts the appointment, the names of the others are put back on the list to be considered for future openings.

That is the rule in hiring from all kinds of eligible lists, whether they are for typist, carpenter, chemist, or something else. For every vacancy, the appointing officer has his choice of any one of the top three eligibles on the list. This explains why the person whose name is on top of the list sometimes does not get an appointment when some of the persons lower on the list do. If the appointing officer chooses the second or third eligible, the No. 1 eligible does not get a job at once, but stays on the list until he is appointed or the list is terminated.

X. HOW TO PASS THE INTERVIEW TEST

The examination for which you applied requires an oral interview test. You have already taken the written test and you are now being called for the interview test – the final part of the formal examination.

You may think that it is not possible to prepare for an interview test and that there are no procedures to follow during an interview. Our purpose is to point out some things you can do in advance that will help you and some good rules to follow and pitfalls to avoid while you are being interviewed.

What is an interview supposed to test?

The written examination is designed to test the technical knowledge and competence of the candidate; the oral is designed to evaluate intangible qualities, not readily measured otherwise, and to establish a list showing the relative fitness of each candidate – as measured against his competitors – for the position sought. Scoring is not on the basis of "right" and "wrong," but on a sliding scale of values ranging from "not passable" to "outstanding." As a matter of fact, it is possible to achieve a relatively low score without a single "incorrect" answer because of evident weakness in the qualities being measured.

Occasionally, an examination may consist entirely of an oral test – either an individual or a group oral. In such cases, information is sought concerning the technical knowledges and abilities of the candidate, since there has been no written examination for this purpose. More commonly, however, an oral test is used to supplement a written examination.

Who conducts interviews?

The composition of oral boards varies among different jurisdictions. In nearly all, a representative of the personnel department serves as chairman. One of the members of the board may be a representative of the department in which the candidate would work. In some cases, "outside experts" are used, and, frequently, a businessman or some other representative of the general public is asked to serve. Labor and management or other special groups may be represented. The aim is to secure the services of experts in the appropriate field.

However the board is composed, it is a good idea (and not at all improper or unethical) to ascertain in advance of the interview who the members are and what groups they represent. When you are introduced to them, you will have some idea of their backgrounds and interests, and at least you will not stutter and stammer over their names.

What should be done before the interview?

While knowledge about the board members is useful and takes some of the surprise element out of the interview, there is other preparation which is more substantive. It *is* possible to prepare for an oral interview – in several ways:

1) Keep a copy of your application and review it carefully before the interview

This may be the only document before the oral board, and the starting point of the interview. Know what education and experience you have listed there, and the sequence and dates of all of it. Sometimes the board will ask you to review the highlights of your experience for them; you should not have to hem and haw doing it.

2) Study the class specification and the examination announcement

Usually, the oral board has one or both of these to guide them. The qualities, characteristics or knowledges required by the position sought are stated in these documents. They offer valuable clues as to the nature of the oral interview. For example, if the job involves supervisory responsibilities, the announcement will usually indicate that knowledge of modern supervisory methods and the qualifications of the candidate as a supervisor will be tested. If so, you can expect such questions, frequently in the form of a hypothetical situation which you are expected to solve. NEVER go into an oral without knowledge of the duties and responsibilities of the job you seek.

3) Think through each qualification required

Try to visualize the kind of questions you would ask if you were a board member. How well could you answer them? Try especially to appraise your own knowledge and background in each area, *measured against the job sought*, and identify any areas in which you are weak. Be critical and realistic – do not flatter yourself.

4) Do some general reading in areas in which you feel you may be weak

For example, if the job involves supervision and your past experience has NOT, some general reading in supervisory methods and practices, particularly in the field of human relations, might be useful. Do NOT study agency procedures or detailed manuals. The oral board will be testing your understanding and capacity, not your memory.

5) Get a good night's sleep and watch your general health and mental attitude

You will want a clear head at the interview. Take care of a cold or any other minor ailment, and of course, no hangovers.

What should be done on the day of the interview?

Now comes the day of the interview itself. Give yourself plenty of time to get there. Plan to arrive somewhat ahead of the scheduled time, particularly if your appointment is in the fore part of the day. If a previous candidate fails to appear, the board might be ready for you a bit early. By early afternoon an oral board is almost invariably behind schedule if there are many candidates, and you may have to wait. Take along a book or magazine to read, or your application to review, but leave any extraneous material in the waiting room when you go in for your interview. In any event, relax and compose yourself.

The matter of dress is important. The board is forming impressions about you – from your experience, your manners, your attitude, and your appearance. Give your personal appearance careful attention. Dress your best, but not your flashiest. Choose conservative, appropriate clothing, and be sure it is immaculate. This is a business interview, and your appearance should indicate that you regard it as such. Besides, being well groomed and properly dressed will help boost your confidence.

Sooner or later, someone will call your name and escort you into the interview room. *This is it.* From here on you are on your own. It is too late for any more preparation. But remember, you asked for this opportunity to prove your fitness, and you are here because your request was granted.

What happens when you go in?

The usual sequence of events will be as follows: The clerk (who is often the board stenographer) will introduce you to the chairman of the oral board, who will introduce you to the other members of the board. Acknowledge the introductions before you sit down. Do not be surprised if you find a microphone facing you or a stenotypist sitting by. Oral interviews are usually recorded in the event of an appeal or other review.

Usually the chairman of the board will open the interview by reviewing the highlights of your education and work experience from your application – primarily for the benefit of the other members of the board, as well as to get the material into the record. Do not interrupt or comment unless there is an error or significant misinterpretation; if that is the case, do not hesitate. But do not quibble about insignificant matters. Also, he will usually ask you some question about your education, experience or your present job – partly to get you to start talking and to establish the interviewing "rapport." He may start the actual questioning, or turn it over to one of the other members. Frequently, each member undertakes the questioning on a particular area, one in which he is perhaps most competent, so you can expect each member to participate in the examination. Because time is limited, you may also expect some rather abrupt switches in the direction the questioning takes, so do not be upset by it. Normally, a board member will not pursue a single line of questioning unless he discovers a particular strength or weakness.

After each member has participated, the chairman will usually ask whether any member has any further questions, then will ask you if you have anything you wish to add. Unless you are expecting this question, it may floor you. Worse, it may start you off on an extended, extemporaneous speech. The board is not usually seeking more information. The question is principally to offer you a last opportunity to present further qualifications or to indicate that you have nothing to add. So, if you feel that a significant qualification or characteristic has been overlooked, it is proper to point it out in a sentence or so. Do not compliment the board on the thoroughness of their examination – they have been sketchy, and you know it. If you wish, merely say, "No thank you, I have nothing further to add." This is a point where you can "talk yourself out" of a good impression or fail to present an important bit of information. Remember, *you close the interview yourself*.

The chairman will then say, "That is all, Mr. _____, thank you." Do not be startled; the interview is over, and quicker than you think. Thank him, gather your belongings and take your leave. Save your sigh of relief for the other side of the door.

How to put your best foot forward
Throughout this entire process, you may feel that the board individually and collectively is trying to pierce your defenses, seek out your hidden weaknesses and embarrass and confuse you. Actually, this is not true. They are obliged to make an appraisal of your qualifications for the job you are seeking, and they want to see you in your best light. Remember, they must interview all candidates and a non-cooperative candidate may become a failure in spite of their best efforts to bring out his qualifications. Here are 15 suggestions that will help you:

1) Be natural – Keep your attitude confident, not cocky
If you are not confident that you can do the job, do not expect the board to be. Do not apologize for your weaknesses, try to bring out your strong points. The board is interested in a positive, not negative, presentation. Cockiness will antagonize any board member and make him wonder if you are covering up a weakness by a false show of strength.

2) Get comfortable, but don't lounge or sprawl
Sit erectly but not stiffly. A careless posture may lead the board to conclude that you are careless in other things, or at least that you are not impressed by the importance of the occasion. Either conclusion is natural, even if incorrect. Do not fuss with your clothing, a pencil or an ashtray. Your hands may occasionally be useful to emphasize a point; do not let them become a point of distraction.

3) Do not wisecrack or make small talk
This is a serious situation, and your attitude should show that you consider it as such. Further, the time of the board is limited – they do not want to waste it, and neither should you.

4) Do not exaggerate your experience or abilities

In the first place, from information in the application or other interviews and sources, the board may know more about you than you think. Secondly, you probably will not get away with it. An experienced board is rather adept at spotting such a situation, so do not take the chance.

5) If you know a board member, do not make a point of it, yet do not hide it

Certainly you are not fooling him, and probably not the other members of the board. Do not try to take advantage of your acquaintanceship – it will probably do you little good.

6) Do not dominate the interview

Let the board do that. They will give you the clues – do not assume that you have to do all the talking. Realize that the board has a number of questions to ask you, and do not try to take up all the interview time by showing off your extensive knowledge of the answer to the first one.

7) Be attentive

You only have 20 minutes or so, and you should keep your attention at its sharpest throughout. When a member is addressing a problem or question to you, give him your undivided attention. Address your reply principally to him, but do not exclude the other board members.

8) Do not interrupt

A board member may be stating a problem for you to analyze. He will ask you a question when the time comes. Let him state the problem, and wait for the question.

9) Make sure you understand the question

Do not try to answer until you are sure what the question is. If it is not clear, restate it in your own words or ask the board member to clarify it for you. However, do not haggle about minor elements.

10) Reply promptly but not hastily

A common entry on oral board rating sheets is "candidate responded readily," or "candidate hesitated in replies." Respond as promptly and quickly as you can, but do not jump to a hasty, ill-considered answer.

11) Do not be peremptory in your answers

A brief answer is proper – but do not fire your answer back. That is a losing game from your point of view. The board member can probably ask questions much faster than you can answer them.

12) Do not try to create the answer you think the board member wants

He is interested in what kind of mind you have and how it works – not in playing games. Furthermore, he can usually spot this practice and will actually grade you down on it.

13) Do not switch sides in your reply merely to agree with a board member

Frequently, a member will take a contrary position merely to draw you out and to see if you are willing and able to defend your point of view. Do not start a debate, yet do not surrender a good position. If a position is worth taking, it is worth defending.

14) Do not be afraid to admit an error in judgment if you are shown to be wrong

The board knows that you are forced to reply without any opportunity for careful consideration. Your answer may be demonstrably wrong. If so, admit it and get on with the interview.

15) Do not dwell at length on your present job

The opening question may relate to your present assignment. Answer the question but do not go into an extended discussion. You are being examined for a *new* job, not your present one. As a matter of fact, try to phrase ALL your answers in terms of the job for which you are being examined.

Basis of Rating

Probably you will forget most of these "do's" and "don'ts" when you walk into the oral interview room. Even remembering them all will not ensure you a passing grade. Perhaps you did not have the qualifications in the first place. But remembering them will help you to put your best foot forward, without treading on the toes of the board members.

Rumor and popular opinion to the contrary notwithstanding, an oral board wants you to make the best appearance possible. They know you are under pressure – but they also want to see how you respond to it as a guide to what your reaction would be under the pressures of the job you seek. They will be influenced by the degree of poise you display, the personal traits you show and the manner in which you respond.

ABOUT THIS BOOK

This book contains tests divided into Examination Sections. Go through each test, answering every question in the margin. We have also attached a sample answer sheet at the back of the book that can be removed and used. At the end of each test look at the answer key and check your answers. On the ones you got wrong, look at the right answer choice and learn. Do not fill in the answers first. Do not memorize the questions and answers, but understand the answer and principles involved. On your test, the questions will likely be different from the samples. Questions are changed and new ones added. If you understand these past questions you should have success with any changes that arise. Tests may consist of several types of questions. We have additional books on each subject should more study be advisable or necessary for you. Finally, the more you study, the better prepared you will be. This book is intended to be the last thing you study before you walk into the examination room. Prior study of relevant texts is also recommended. NLC publishes some of these in our Fundamental Series. Knowledge and good sense are important factors in passing your exam. Good luck also helps. So now study this Passbook, absorb the material contained within and take that knowledge into the examination. Then do your best to pass that exam.

EXAMINATION SECTION

EXAMINATION SECTION
TEST 1

DIRECTIONS: Each question or incomplete statement is followed by several suggested answers or completions. Select the one that BEST answers the question or completes the statement. *PRINT THE LETTER OF THE CORRECT ANSWER IN THE SPACE AT THE RIGHT.*

1. Ebenezer Howard is BEST known for the concept of self-sufficient towns with mixed economies which are called

    A. new towns
    B. garden cities
    C. planned unit developments
    D. suburbs

2. The new town of Columbia, Maryland, has which of the following planned features?
    I. Neighborhood clusters
    II. A rail commuter system
    III. Prior land assembly
    IV. Prohibition of industry
   The CORRECT answer is:

    A. II *only*   B. I, III   C. II, IV   D. I, III, IV

3. The two lines on the graph shown at the right BEST represent which of the following combinations of travel behavior in a metropolitan area of 2 million population?

    A. Transit and private automobile trips
    B. Weekday and weekend trips
    C. All work and nonwork trips
    D. Office and retail-generated trips

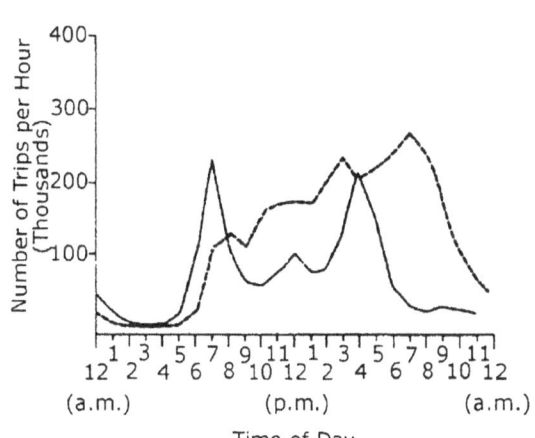

4. Assume that you are the director of a local planning agency, and that you recognize the interdependency of the chief executive, the planning agency, operating departments, and independent boards and commissions. In a hypothetical situation, a proposed expansion of a county airport and adjacent industrial areas is in opposition to the planning agency's proposal for a regional park location.
   The planning agency believes there are unique circumstances and sound reasons for preferring the regional park proposal along with future relocation of the airport to another site in the county.
   Which of the following strategies would likely place you, as the planning director, in the LEAST effective coordinating role in resolving the conflict?

A. Attempting to have the planning agency solely responsible for additional studies and recommendations
B. Directing planning staff to discontinue all studies of this issue and direct all inquiries regarding this matter to the director
C. Recommending the study control be given to the staff of the chief executive's office
D. Soliciting support of other departments and agencies for the planning agency's regional park proposal

5. Recent major developments in household characteristics in the United States have been characterized by which of the following? 5.____
   I. A marked increase in nonfamily living arrangements among the adult population has been observed in recent years.
   II. A major development in marriage trends has been the sharply decreasing level of divorce in central cities.
   III. Families (households where all members are related) maintained by either men or women who have no spouse living with them represent a growing proportion of all family households.
   IV. After several decades of decline in household size, the number of persons per unit has increased in metropolitan area since 1970.

   The CORRECT answer is:

   A. I only   B. I, III   C. III, IV   D. I, II, IV

Questions 6-9.

DIRECTIONS: The group of questions below consists of four lettered headings followed by a list of numbered phrases. For each numbered phrase, select the one heading which is MOST closely related to it. One heading may be used once, more than once, or not at all.

In the following list, which of the formal bodies that operate within a city most likely would take final action on each of the following requests?

   A. City Council
   B. City Court
   C. Board of Zoning Appeals
   D. School Board

6. A request to acquire land for a new school. 6.____

7. A request to condemn property in a blighted area. 7.____

8. A request to levy a special property assessment for a street. 8.____

9. A request for a variance from a zoning ordinance. 9.____

10. In reference to the following hypothetical linear regression equation that describes household trip generation with the census tract as the unit of analysis, which of the following statements about R^2 is CORRECT?

    $T = -.65 + .96(p) + .61(v)$
    $R^2 = .69$
    T = the average number of daily vehicle trips from home per DU (dwelling unit)
    p = persons per DU
    v = vehicles per DU

    A. It shows that more p causes households to make more trips.
    B. It shows that more p, only when coupled with more automobiles, causes households to make more trips.
    C. It indicates that 69% of the variation in trip generation is explained by p and v.
    D. There is a 45% probability that the variables T, p, and v are correlated by chance.

Questions 11-14.

DIRECTIONS: Questions 11 through 14 are to be answered on the basis of the following circumstance.

The desirability and feasibility of a proposed shopping center are to be evaluated. The primary concerns are that conditions of the city zoning ordinance be met and that the project be a profitable venture. The developer owns a 30-acre parcel and proposes to construct a 250,000-square foot leasable area with 1,300 on-site parking spaces. The shopping center will serve a trade area that contains 20,000 households. The average household disposable income is $12,000. The shopping center will have a 50:50 split of square footage between convenience and shopper's goods.

11. Which of the following would be APPROPRIATE in a shopping center of this size?

    A. A major grocery and a drugstore as prime tenants
    B. Either a department or discount store as the anchor tenant
    C. Three department stores of approximately the same size
    D. A series of smaller stores rather than an anchor tenant

12. If an average of 400 square feet is needed to accommodate each parking space and associated driveways, the APPROXIMATE acreage of the blacktop area of the site would be _____ acres.

    A. Less than 10   B. Between 10 and 15
    C. Between 15 and 20   D. More than 20

13. If 50 percent of disposable income is allocated to retail purchases, a minimum of $100 of sales per square foot is needed to operate profitably, and 750,000 square feet of retail business already exists in the trade area, which of the following should be concluded? The

    A. trade area is already overbuilt and cannot support additional development without further population growth
    B. new shopping center will use up all of the untapped purchasing power of the trade area

C. existing and proposed centers can operate profitably with excess purchasing power available for additional development
D. trade area is not overbuilt presently, but it can only accommodate an additional 150,000 square feet

14. Provisions in the zoning ordinance require a 4:1 ratio of open space to building space and a 5:1,000-square foot ratio of parking space to gross leasable area (GLA). According to the ordinance, which of the following statements about the parcel is CORRECT?
It is

   A. too small to accommodate the projected center, although adequate parking would be provided
   B. large enough to accommodate the projected center, but parking spaces would be inadequate
   C. large enough to accommodate the projected center, and sufficient parking would be provided
   D. grossly underutilized and could accommodate additional square footage and additional parking spaces

Questions 15-17.

DIRECTIONS: Questions 15 through 17 are to be answered on the basis of the following information.

Planners in a large city that consists of 150 neighborhoods are concerned about the provision and allocation of health-care clinics at the multiple-neighborhood level throughout the city. One of the main concerns is prenatal health care. Variables relevant to this situation are as follows:

QPNHC = the overall quality of prenatal health care
IMR = the percentage of children who survive their first three months of life (a type of infant mortality rate) and who were born in the same one-year period
NWP = the number of women pregnant at any time during a one-year period
NA = the number of appointments kept at the health clinic per year
FI = the family incomes of residents in thousands of dollars ($1,000's)
D = the distance of families from the health clinics in miles

(Neighborhood averages can be generated for each of these variables.)

15. The planners have decided that the neighborhood infant mortality rate will serve as the operational objective of the prenatal health care system.
Which of the following would be the MOST serious criticism leveled against their decision?

   A. It is impossible to calculate the IMR at the neighborhood level.
   B. The data on the use of the clinic (NA) are easier to obtain and more accurate than the other data.
   C. The IMR is a good quantitative but weak qualitative index of the QPNHC.
   D. The collection of IMR data is irrelevant to the problem.

16. Which of the following is an output variable within the model?

   A. IMR   B. NWP   C. FI   D. D

17. It is now 10 years later; the clinics were built and a very comprehensive data collection system was kept in operation. The clinic programs are under fire, the budgets are expected to be slashed, and some clinics probably will be forced to close. Time is short. Based on this situation, which of the following would be the LEAST critical evaluation question?   17.____

    A. Are higher levels of clinic usage associated with various infant mortality rates?
    B. If distance does not affect the use of the clinics, does it do so differentially by income strata?
    C. What kinds of persons (education, income level, etc.) use each clinic?
    D. Are family income levels associated with distance

KEY (CORRECT ANSWERS)

1. B
2. B
3. C
4. B
5. B

6. D
7. A
8. A
9. C
10. C

11. B
12. B
13. C
14. C
15. C
16. A
17. D

EXAMINATION SECTION
TEST 1

DIRECTIONS: Each question or incomplete statement is followed by several suggested answers or completions. Select the one that BEST answers the question or completes the statement. *PRINT THE LETTER OF THE CORRECT ANSWER IN THE SPACE AT THE RIGHT.*

Questions 1-5.

DIRECTIONS: Questions 1 through 5 are based on the table shown below.

POPULATION, URBAN AND RURAL, BY RACE: 2000 TO 2020

In thousands, except percent. An urbanized area comprises at least 1 city of 50,000 inhabitants (central city) plus contiguous, closely settled areas (urban fringe). Data for 2000 and 2010 according to urban definition used in the 2010 census; 2020 data according to the 2020 definition.

YEAR AND AREA	TOTAL	WHITE	ALL OTHER	PERCENT DISTRIBUTION		
				TOTAL	WHITE	ALL OTHER
2000, total population	151,326	135,150	16,176	100.0	100.0	100.0
Urban	96,847	86,864	9,983	64.0	64.3	61.7
Inside urbanized areas	69,249	61,925	7,324	45.8	45.8	45.3
Central cities	48,377	42,042	6,335	32.0	31.1	39.2
Urban fringe	20,872	19,883	989	13.8	14.7	6.1
Outside urbanized areas	27,598	24,939	2,659	18.2	18.5	16.4
Rural	54,479	48,286	6,193	36.0	35.7	38.3
2010, total population	179,323	158,832	20,491	100.0	100.0	100.0
Urban	125,269	110,428	14,840	69.9	69.5	72.4
Inside urbanized areas	95,848	83,770	12,079	53.5	52.7	58.9
Central cities	57,975	47,627	10,348	32.3	30.0	50.5
Urban fringe	37,873	36,143	1,371	21.1	22.8	8.4
Outside urbanized areas	29,420	26,658	2,762	16.4	16.8	13.5
Rural	54,054	48,403	5,651	30.1	30.5	27.6
2020, total population	203,212	177,749	25,463	100.0	100.0	100.0
Urban	149,325	128,773	20,552	73.5	72.4	80.7
Inside urbanized areas	118,447	100,952	17,495	58.3	56.8	68.7
Central cities	63,922	49,547	14,375	31.5	27.9	56.5
Urban fringe	54,525	51,405	3,120	26.8	28.9	12.3
Outside urbanized areas	30,878	27,822	3,057	15.2	15.7	12.0
Rural	53,887	48,976	4,911	26.5	27.6	19.3

1. The ratio of urban to rural population in 2000 was MOST NEARLY   1.____

   A. 3:1   B. 4:1   C. 2:1   D. 14:1

2. According to the table, the trend of population inside urban areas has been   2.____

   A. towards greater concentration   B. towards less concentration
   C. towards stabilization   D. erratic

3. Since 2000, the urban fringe white population has substantially increased while the urban fringe other population has

   A. slightly decreased
   B. greatly decreased
   C. remained the same
   D. increased moderately

4. Over the years, the percentage of the urban white population as compared with the percentage of the total urban population has

   A. remained relatively constant
   B. substantially decreased
   C. substantially increased
   D. varied

5. Select the one of the following which BEST describes the central city white population rate of decrease since 2000 as compared with the central city black population rate of increase.

   A. The central city white population rate of decrease has been greater than the central city black population rate of increase.
   B. The central city white and black populations have not increased to a significant degree.
   C. The central city white population rate of decrease has been equal to the central city black population rate of increase.
   D. The central city white population rate of decrease has been less than the central city black population rate of increase.

Questions 6-10.

DIRECTIONS: Questions 6 through 10 are to be answered on the basis of the table shown below.

STANDARDS FOR RECREATION AREAS

TYPE OF AREA	ACRES PER 1,000 POPULATION	SIZE OF SITE (ACRES) IDEAL	SIZE OF SITE (ACRES) MINIMUM	RADIUS OF AREA SERVED (MILES)
Playgrounds	1.5	4	2	0.5
Neighborhood parks	2.0	10	5	0.5
Playfields	1.5	15	10	1.5
Community parks	3.5	100	40	2.0
District parks	2.0	200	100	3.0
Regional parks and reservations	15.0	500-1,000	varies	10.0

6. What is the MINIMUM number of playfields that a community of 15,000 people may contain if the size of each is kept within the limits shown in the table?

   A. 4   B. 10   C. 6   D. 2

7. If, as far as possible, ideal sized playgrounds are built, how many IDEAL SIZED playgrounds should a community of 12,000 people contain?

   A. 4   B. 8   C. 1   D. 10

8. Approximately how many people can a community park of 200 acres serve? 8._____

   A. 120,000   B. 80,000   C. 55,000   D. 20,000

9. If only minimum sized neighborhood parks are built, how many will be required for a population of 20,000? 9._____

   A. 5   B. 2   C. 8   D. 12

10. A community of 75,000 persons is evenly distributed over a 5 square mile area. Of the following, the number and size of playgrounds that would BEST satisfy the standards is _____ playgrounds @ _____ acres each. 10._____

    A. 5; 7.5   B. 35; 3.5   C. 10; 10   D. 50; 1.5

11. The illustration shown at the right is an example of a 11._____

    A. simple grade separation
    B. simple interchange of a freeway with a highway
    C. three-level interchange
    D. T interchange

12. The practical MINIMUM number of cars per hour that can be carried per lane on a limited access roadway with uninterrupted flow is considered to be APPROXIMATELY 12._____

    A. 750   B. 1,500   C. 5,000   D. 10,000

13. A street that is open at only one end, with provision for a turn-around at the other, is called a 13._____

    A. local street   B. cul-de-sac
    C. loop street   D. minor street

14. Which of the following shopping center types is the local source of staple goods and daily services? 14._____

    A. Central Business District
    B. Regional Shopping Center
    C. Highway Strip Development
    D. Neighborhood Shopping Center

15. *Air rights* refers to the concept that 15._____

    A. all people are entitled to clean air
    B. vistas from apartments cannot be obstructed
    C. buildings can be constructed over railroads or highways
    D. buildings should be oriented towards the prevailing breezes

16. The one of the following LEAST likely to be considered an integral part of urban design is 16._____

    A. spatial forms   B. surfaces
    C. vistas   D. underground utilities

Questions 17-21.

DIRECTIONS: Questions 17 through 21 are based upon the table shown below.

LIVE BIRTHS, DEATHS, MARRIAGES, AND DIVORCES: 1940-1991

	Number (1,000)				Rate per 1,000 Population				
		DEATHS		MAR-	DIVOR-		DEATHS		MAR-	DIVOR-
YEAR	BIRTHS	TOTAL	INFANT	RIAGES	CES	BIRTHS	TOTAL	INFANT	RIAGES	CES
1940	2,777	697	(NA)	948	83	30.1	14.7	(NA)	10.3	0.9
1945	2,965	816	78	1,008	104	29.5	13.2	99.9	10.0	1.0
1950	2,950	1,118	130	1,274	171	27.7	13.0	85.8	12.0	1.6
1955	2,909	1,192	135	1,188	175	25.1	11.7	71.7	10.3	1.5
1960	2,618	1,327	142	1,127	196	21.3	11.3	64.6	9.2	1.6
1965	2,377	1,393	120	1,327	218	18.7	10.9	55.7	10.4	1.7
1970	2,559	1,417	111	1,596	264	19.4	10.8	47.0	12.1	2.0
1975	2,858	1,402	105	1,613	485	20.4	10.6	38.3	12.2	3.5
1980	3,632	1,452	104	1,667	385	24.1	9.6	29.2	11.1	2.6
1985	4,104	1,529	107	1,531	377	25.0	9.3	26.4	9.3	2.3
1990	4,258	1,712	111	1,523	393	23.7	9.5	26.0	8.5	2.2
1991	4,268	1,702	108	1,548	414	23.3	9.3	25.3	8.5	2.3

NA   Not Available

17. From 1940 to 1991, the birth rate has

    A. approximately doubled
    B. remained stable
    C. been reduced by 25%
    D. had two breaks in its downward progression

18. A comparison of the total population death rate to the infant death rate shows that

    A. the two rates have remained constant
    B. the infant death rate is greater
    C. the total population death rate has decreased at a faster rate
    D. infants had a greater chance to survive in 1965 than in 1980

19. In 1945, about one marriage out of 10 ended in divorce.
    In which of the following years would the rate be LESS?

    A. 1985   B. 1965   C. 1950   D. 1940

20. The significance of the decrease in the infant death rate is that

    A. family size will increase
    B. family size will decrease
    C. family size will not be affected
    D. children will become a smaller percentage of the total population

21. According to the chart, the total death rate declined from 14.7 in 1940 to 9.3 in 1991, yet each year more people have died. This fact is MOST likely accounted for by

    A. poor reporting techniques
    B. the decrease in the mortality rate
    C. the increase of total population
    D. the increase of older people in the total population

22. The type of interchange pictured in the illustration shown at the right is called a _____ interchange.

    A. simple
    B. cloverleaf
    C. universal
    D. Bel Geddes

22._____

23. This type of interchange (pictured in the preceding question) is used when

    A. topographic conditions are difficult
    B. traffic volumes are heavy
    C. a major and minor road intersect
    D. two major roads intersect

23._____

24. The one of the following basic requirements which would NOT be considered an integral part of a comprehensive plan is

    A. a capital improvement program
    B. physical design proposals
    C. long-range policy statements
    D. social and economic considerations

24._____

Questions 25-28.

DIRECTIONS: Questions 25 through 28 are based on the data shown below, which indicates total housing units.

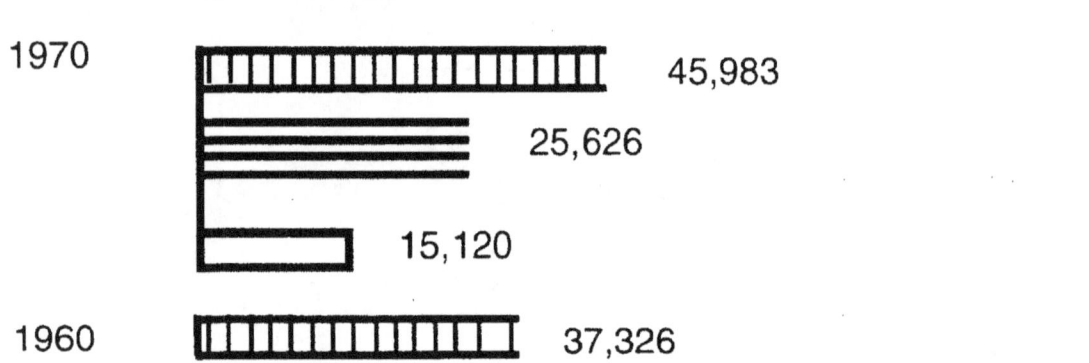

HOUSING UNITS: 1960 to 1990
NUMBER IN THOUSANDS

▥ TOTAL   ≡ INSIDE SMSA'S   ☐ IN CENTRAL CITIES

(SMSA's = Standard Metropolitan Statistical Areas)

1990: 68,679 / 46,295 / 22,594
1980: 58,326 / 36,386 / 19,622
1970: 45,983 / 25,626 / 15,120
1960: 37,326

25. The period of GREATEST production of housing units was

A. 1950-60   B. 1980-90   C. 1970-80   D. 1960-70

26. The location of the LARGEST gains in housing units since 1960 was in the

A. suburban areas   B. central cities
C. SMSA's   D. rural areas

27. Contrary to many misconceptions, the above data shows that the central cities are

A. losing population to the suburbs
B. keeping pace with the overall housing development
C. showing strong development trends
D. growing, but at a decreasing rate

28. Based on the above data, which of the following statements is MOST accurate? 28.____

    A. The housing stock is rapidly becoming outdated.
    B. More new homes are located in suburban areas than in central cities.
    C. The housing supply is rapidly catching up to the demand.
    D. The majority of the population is located in the SMSA's.

29. The name of the long-range schedule of major projects and their estimated costs over a period of 5-10 years is the 29.____

    A. budget
    B. comprehensive plan
    C. capital improvement program
    D. input-output program

30. *Cost Benefit Analysis* is a method used to 30.____

    A. determine budget compliance
    B. compare costs and benefits of a particular investment
    C. evaluate productivity in school construction
    D. establish social benefits for a neighborhood

31. A *workable program* is a SIGNIFICANT element of a(n) 31.____

    A. urban renewal program
    B. comprehensive plan
    C. capital improvement program
    D. urban design program

32. Which of the following would NOT be considered a major type of municipal planning agency in the United States? 32.____

    A. An independent planning commission
    B. The planning department
    C. A community development department
    D. A local renewal agency

33. Townhouses are MOST closely related to which of the following types of residential construction? 33.____

    A. Garden apartments   B. Row houses
    C. High-rise complexes   D. Semi-attached houses

34. The one of the following which could NOT be considered an accessory use in a residence district is a 34.____

    A. garage   B. greenhouse
    C. dwelling   D. storage shed

35. The ratio of parking space to retail floor area in a major regional shopping center would MOST often be 35.____

    A. 1:1   B. 3:1   C. 6:1   D. 10:1

KEY (CORRECT ANSWERS)

1.	C	16.	D
2.	A	17.	C
3.	D	18.	B
4.	A	19.	D
5.	D	20.	C
6.	D	21.	C
7.	A	22.	B
8.	C	23.	D
9.	C	24.	A
10.	B	25.	C
11.	A	26.	A
12.	B	27.	D
13.	B	28.	B
14.	D	29.	C
15.	C	30.	B

31. A
32. D
33. B
34. C
35. B

TEST 2

DIRECTIONS: Each question or incomplete statement is followed by several suggested answers or completions. Select the one that BEST answers the question or completes the statement. *PRINT THE LETTER OF THE CORRECT ANSWER IN THE SPACE AT THE RIGHT.*

1. When the term *density* is commonly employed as a measure of land use, it refers to the   1._____

    A. number of persons B. land coverage
    C. number of buildings D. number of dwelling units

2. The *City Beautiful* movement was an outgrowth of the   2._____

    A. Bauhaus School in 1920
    B. Chicago World's Fair in 1893
    C. N.Y.C. Zoning Ordinance of 1916
    D. planning concepts of Emilio Sitte

3. The American Greenbelt towns were built to   3._____

    A. create open space
    B. establish independent satellite communities
    C. establish residential *dormitory* communities
    D. disperse urban population

4. The FIRST United States Housing Act was passed by Congress in   4._____

    A. 1929   B. 1949   C. 1941   D. 1937

5. A specific ratio of permissible floor space to lot area is known as   5._____

    A. floor area ratio B. open space ratio
    C. sky exposure plane D. lot coverage

6. A *protective covenant* can BEST be described as a(n)   6._____

    A. zoning ordinance B. easement
    C. fire insurance policy D. deed restriction

7. Underground utility lines are PREFERRED by most planners rather than overhead lines because underground lines   7._____

    A. are more accessible for maintenance
    B. cost less
    C. are not visible
    D. are laid in proper easements

8. If a local street right-of-way is 50 feet, the paved width of the street is GENERALLY _____ feet.   8._____

    A. 18   B. 26   C. 44   D. 50

9. The term *zero population growth* refers to the concept that

   A. the population will eventually become extinct
   B. married couples will not bear children
   C. each family will produce only two children
   D. parents will be subject to a planned schedule of parenthood

10. The MOST common dimensions of a half-acre residential lot are

    A. 100 ft. x 100 ft.
    B. 100 ft. x 200 ft.
    C. 120 ft. x 150 ft.
    D. 200 ft. x 200 ft.

11. As a general rule, large street trees should be planted

    A. 25 feet apart
    B. 50-75 feet apart
    C. 150-200 feet apart
    D. spaced randomly

12. A key regulation of a zoning ordinance relates to the

    A. architectural style of a building
    B. slope of a site
    C. height and bulk of buildings
    D. subsoil conditions

13. Under which one of the following authorities are zoning ordinances adopted by local communities?

    A. Police power
    B. Community power
    C. Will of the people
    D. Common law

14. MOST state enabling laws require that zoning regulations be based upon a

    A. land use plan
    B. base map
    C. comprehensive plan
    D. topographical map

15. The OBJECTIVE of an *interim zoning ordinance* is to

    A. zone only a portion of the community for a special purpose
    B. maintain existing conditions until a more comprehensive ordinance is prepared
    C. create a special district
    D. allow greater freedom in interpretation and utilization of the zoning regulations

16. A *non-conforming* use is

    A. a use which requires special approval to remain
    B. a building that does not comply with yard or bulk regulations
    C. one that is not permitted in a specific district
    D. a building which is structurally unsafe

17. A variance is granted by a board of appeals to

    A. obtain financial relief
    B. provide a balance of power
    C. test community opinion
    D. relieve practical difficulty and hardship

18. Which of the following zoning regulations, taken by itself, would permit the MOST floor area of building on a specific lot?
A

    A. floor area ratio of 3:1
    B. maximum lot coverage of 60%
    C. maximum building height of 50 feet
    D. parking ratio of 2:1

19. Sewers used to carry rain or surface water to a body of water so as to prevent flooding are called _____ sewers.

    A. sanitary   B. storm   C. combined   D. overflow

20. The *Garden City* concept was made famous through a book written by

    A. Sir Patrick Abercombie
    B. Patrick Geddes
    C. Ebenezer Howard
    D. Sir Raymond Unwin

21. *Broadacre City* was advocated as a concept of urban development by

    A. F.L. Wright
    B. Corbusier
    C. Saarinen
    D. Geddes

22. The man who can BEST be associated with the planning principle of *high density-low coverage* is

    A. Wright
    B. VanderRohe
    C. Saarinen
    D. Corbusier

23. The AVERAGE number of persons per household in the United States in 1970 was MOST NEARLY

    A. 2.0   B. 2.5   C. 3.0   D. 3.5

24. Which of the following methods would be the MOST accurate in making population projections?

    A. Migration and natural increase
    B. Apportionment
    C. School enrollment
    D. Geometric extrapolation

25. According to the 1990 census, the total population of the United States was MOST NEARLY _____ million persons.

    A. 190   B. 200   C. 280   D. 350

26. After the amounts of different land uses in a medium-size city have been tabulated, which of the following percentages of the total developed land would USUALLY be utilized for streets?

    A. 12%   B. 20%   C. 30%   D. 8%

27. During the past twenty years, the MOST significant factor causing reorientation of traditional urban land use patterns has been

   A. express highway construction
   B. airport development
   C. new schools
   D. permissive zoning ordinances

28. The fundamental objective of MOST suburban communities in attracting new industries is to

   A. increase local employment opportunities
   B. attract minority groups to relocate
   C. establish a balanced land use pattern
   D. increase tax income

29. Which of the following terms is NOT considered to be part of the street classification system?

   A. Major street
   B. Right-of-way
   C. Local street
   D. Cul-de-sac

30. The USUAL purpose for providing a water tower in a municipal water supply system is to

   A. establish a constant pressure
   B. increase the supply of water
   C. increase water pressure
   D. provide a reserve supply

31. The neighborhood unit concept, which includes the elementary school as its major element, was FIRST advocated in 1929 by

   A. Clarence Stein
   B. Henry Wright
   C. Clarence Perry
   D. N. Engelhardt

32. In the past few years, the type of housing which has received the LEAST amount of consideration in resolving the housing problem is

   A. cluster housing
   B. urban renewal
   C. public housing
   D. middle-income housing

33. *Performance standards* have become an INTEGRAL part of zoning ordinances relating to

   A. road construction
   B. industrial districts
   C. parking garages
   D. commercial areas

34. The legal concept upon which the exercise of *condemnation* is based is called the

   A. *due process* clause of the Constitution
   B. police power
   C. power of eminent domain
   D. general community welfare

35. In which of the following situations would the granting of a zoning variance be considered as IMPROPER action? A(n)

   A. serious topographic condition
   B. undersized lot held prior to zoning
   C. subsurface water condition
   D. economic loss due to a zone change

KEY (CORRECT ANSWERS)

1. D
2. B
3. C
4. D
5. A

6. D
7. C
8. B
9. C
10. B

11. B
12. C
13. A
14. C
15. B

16. C
17. D
18. B
19. B
20. C

21. A
22. D
23. B
24. A
25. C

26. C
27. A
28. D
29. B
30. A

31. C
32. C
33. B
34. C
35. D

TEST 3

DIRECTIONS: Each question or incomplete statement is followed by several suggested answers or completions. Select the one that BEST answers the question or completes the statement. *PRINT THE LETTER OF THE CORRECT ANSWER IN THE SPACE AT THE RIGHT.*

1. The MAJOR objective of cluster zoning is to provide

   A. greater densities
   B. a variety of housing types
   C. open space
   D. racial balance

2. One tool in combating the problems of *spread city* is to provide

   A. improved mass transportation systems
   B. more major highways
   C. more single-family detached houses
   D. more community facilities

3. The Environmental Protection Agency has issued national air quality standards for six common pollutants. The one of the following pollutants NOT included is

   A. sulfur oxides
   B. carbon monoxide
   C. sulfur dioxide
   D. hydrocarbon oxides

4. The national air quality standards have been issued in two parts: primary and secondary standards. A PRIMARY standard is designed to

   A. protect public health
   B. protect public welfare
   C. establish ambient air quality
   D. prevent damage to the environment

5. The MAJOR source of air pollution in many urban areas, according to the Environmental Protection Agency, is

   A. emissions from new plants
   B. fossil-fueled steam-generating plants
   C. motor vehicles
   D. large incinerators

6. A technique designed for the analysis of national economies and which employs an industry interaction model appearing in the form of a multi-sector or industrial matrix is called

   A. economic base theory
   B. industrial complex analysis
   C. calculated forecasting
   D. input-output theory

7. The traditional master plan, with its strong emphasis on physical improvements, is being more frequently replaced by

   A. policies planning
   B. normative planning
   C. quantitative analysis
   D. flexible planning

8. *Advocate planning* involves the planner in

   A. participating on a federal level to influence local officials
   B. working within the planning unit to obtain his desired goals
   C. working as a citizen, often as a protagonist against the local government
   D. preparing mathematical models of urban development

9. Of the following, the type of commercial development which is LEAST likely to be planned is a

   A. regional shopping center
   B. local shopping complex
   C. highway strip development
   D. central business district

10. The *official map* of a community designates all of the following EXCEPT

    A. street right-of-ways
    B. parks and playgrounds
    C. residential areas
    D. school sites

11. Land use intensity standards are MOST appropriately utilized with the development of

    A. standard subdivisions
    B. planned unit developments
    C. mobile home parks
    D. high-rise residential complexes

12. A topographic map does NOT generally express

    A. climatic conditions
    B. easements
    C. boundary lines and distances
    D. existing buildings

13. Clarence Stein contributed GREATLY to the development of

    A. the concept of the balanced community
    B. the design of Reston
    C. high-rise residential complexes
    D. the Radburn Plan

14. In site development, a 10% grade is considered MAXIMUM for

    A. streets and roads
    B. play fields
    C. building sites
    D. parking lots

15. The Model Cities Program includes all of the following EXCEPT

    A. job training in construction work
    B. local control of programs
    C. physical and social rehabilitation of a community
    D. new city design and development

16. HUD's *Operation Breakthrough* program encouraged

    A. fireproof buildings
    B. innovative prefabricated systems of construction
    C. speed of building erection
    D. a socio-economic assault on the housing program

17. A condominium can BEST be described as a

    A. high-rise residential complex with a complete range of amenities
    B. variation of cooperative ownership
    C. planned unit development with open space
    D. building with full ownership of the dwelling unit and common ownership of public areas

18. A MAJOR advantage of a leaching cesspool is that it

    A. can be used where ground water is two feet below grade
    B. can be used close to potable water
    C. requires a minimum of land area
    D. is limited in capacity

19. Land which rises 2 feet vertically to 5 feet horizontally has a slope of

    A. 2.5%   B. 20%   C. 25%   D. 40%

20. The MAJOR advantage of a subsoil disposal bed for sewage disposal is that it

    A. may be used in any soil except that rated as impervious
    B. is more economical to build
    C. requires less land area than that of a treatment plant
    D. may have a ground water level less than 2 feet below grade

21. To achieve the GREATEST amount of open space in the siting of houses, the one of the following patterns that a planner would MOST probably choose is a _____ pattern.

    A. gridiron   B. court
    C. cluster   D. free-form

22. The maximum distance a child should be required to walk to an elementary school is GENERALLY considered to be _____ mile.

    A. 1/4   B. 1/2   C. 3/4   D. 1

23. Modern industrial parks most often will include all of the following amenities EXCEPT   23._____

    A. landscaping and screening
    B. employee parking areas
    C. utilities and services
    D. multi-story structures

24. The BEST source of aerial photographs that provide the greatest coverage of the United States by a single agency is the   24._____

    A. Soil Conservation Service
    B. U.S. National Ocean Survey
    C. National Park Service
    D. Agricultural Stabilization Conservation Service

25. Terrain analysis is MOST closely related to the study of   25._____

    A. landforms
    B. drainage
    C. soil
    D. land erosion

26. Riparian rights deal with property that is located   26._____

    A. over mineral resources
    B. along a body of water
    C. over railroad tracks
    D. over a right-of-way

27. The ADVANTAGE of a *stol* port is that it   27._____

    A. can be located near another airport
    B. is not government regulated
    C. accommodates business and pleasure aircraft
    D. requires a short runway

28. One square mile contains EXACTLY _____ acres.   28._____

    A. 316   B. 444   C. 640   D. 1,000

29. The one of the following methods of refuse disposal that causes the LEAST air pollution, if efficiently carried out, is   29._____

    A. open dumping
    B. land fill
    C. incineration
    D. compositing

30. Sewers which collect sewage only from the plumbing systems of buildings and carry it to a sewage treatment plant are called _____ sewers.   30._____

    A. sanitary
    B. storm
    C. combined
    D. constant-flow

KEY (CORRECT ANSWERS)

1.	C	16.	B
2.	A	17.	D
3.	C	18.	C
4.	A	19.	D
5.	C	20.	A
6.	D	21.	C
7.	A	22.	B
8.	C	23.	D
9.	C	24.	D
10.	C	25.	A
11.	B	26.	B
12.	A	27.	D
13.	D	28.	C
14.	A	29.	B
15.	D	30.	A

EXAMINATION SECTION
TEST 1

DIRECTIONS: Each question or incomplete statement is followed by several suggested, answers or completions. Select the one that BEST answers the question or completes the statement. *PRINT THE LETTER OF THE CORRECT ANSWER IN THE SPACE AT THE RIGHT.*

1. The authority to establish zoning ordinances by a community comes from

    A. the police power of the state
    B. local determination
    C. the federal government
    D. implied powers of the community

    1.____

2. On a land use map, the standard color used to designate residential use is

    A. green   B. blue   C. purple   D. yellow

    2.____

3. In population analysis, a population pyramid indicates

    A. male and female age groupings
    B. total population projections
    C. fertility ratios
    D. educational achievements

    3.____

4. The determination of a standard metropolitan statistical area is established by

    A. local considerations   B. regional agencies
    C. the U.S. Census Bureau   D. state agencies

    4.____

5. The population census of the United States is taken every _____ years.

    A. 2   B. 4   C. 5   D. 10

    5.____

6. There are strong indications that planning agencies are developing a new approach to the traditional methods of city planning.
This new approach is called

    A. advocacy planning
    B. long-range physical planning
    C. community development
    D. policies planning

    6.____

7. A key element of a comprehensive plan for a community is the

    A. zoning ordinance   B. land use plan
    C. official map   D. subdivision regulation

    7.____

8. The official map of a community is a document that

    A. shows population projections and educational trends
    B. pinpoints the location of future streets and other public facilities
    C. identifies capital improvements and budgets
    D. indicates all community facilities

    8.____

9. During the past decade, planning programs generally have become increasingly concerned with which one of the following?

   A. Long-range physical design
   B. Highway locations
   C. Social welfare
   D. Natural resources

10. The city planning process encompasses several basic phases. Which one of the following phases would NOT be considered typical?

    A. Cost-benefit analysis
    B. Goal formulation
    C. Data collection and research
    D. Plan preparation and programming

11. The MOST common use of easements in new housing subdivisions is for

    A. air rights
    B. utilities
    C. open space
    D. absorption fields

12. The phrase *non-complying use* relates to which one of the following regulations?

    A. Zoning Ordinance
    B. Building Code
    C. Subdivision regulations
    D. Health Code

13. Performance standards are generally associated with which one of the following types of zoning districts?

    A. Residential
    B. Commercial
    C. Manufacturing
    D. Flood plain

14. The PRIMARY goal of cluster-type development is to

    A. increase population density
    B. insure open space
    C. discourage rapid development
    D. bypass zoning requirements

15. Which of the following is MOST closely related to the land-use intensity standards developed by the Federal Housing Administration?

    A. Quality of housing
    B. Planned unit development
    C. Low-cost housing
    D. Land management policy

16. If the density of a residential subdivision is 8 dwelling units per acre, then the average size lot should be APPROXIMATELY

    A. 25 ft. x 100 ft.
    B. 55 ft. x 100 ft.
    C. 100 ft. x 100 ft.
    D. 200 ft. x 200 ft.

17. In planning the open parking area for community facilities, the amount of space allocated per care should be APPROXIMATELY _____ sq.ft.

    A. 150   B. 300   C. 600   D. 800

18. Which of the following facilities would be MOST appropriate on the roof of a building?   18.____

    A. Stolport   B. Heliport
    C. Airport   D. Cargo port

19. Sanitary landfill is a method of   19.____

    A. sewage disposal   B. composting
    C. incineration   D. refuse disposal

20. Which of the following is NOT considered to be an air pollutant by the Environmental Protection Agency?   20.____

    A. Nitrates   B. Sulfur oxides
    C. Carbon monoxide   D. Hydrocarbons

21. Which of the following recreation facilities is NOT considered a typical neighborhood facility?   21.____

    A. Tot lot   B. Playground
    C. Wading pool   D. Playfield

22. Which of the following methods would be the MOST accurate in making a population projection for a small community?   22.____

    A. Migration and natural increase
    B. Apportionment and voting records
    C. School enrollment and housing starts
    D. Geometric extrapolation

23. When a planning map is to be reproduced to different sizes, the map scale should be expressed   23.____

    A. mathematically   B. in graphic form
    C. in feet and inches D. by metes and bounds

24. The one of the following characteristics which is NOT typical of new industrial parks is   24.____

    A. off-street loading   B. extensive landscaping
    C. employee parking   D. 2-story structures

25. A greenbelt surrounding a community can be used for many activities.
    The one of the following activities LEAST appropriate for greenbelt use is   25.____

    A. farming   B. recreation
    C. local shopping   D. flood plain control

KEY (CORRECT ANSWERS)

1. A
2. D
3. A
4. C
5. D

6. D
7. B
8. B
9. C
10. A

11. B
12. A
13. C
14. B
15. B

16. B
17. B
18. B
19. D
20. A

21. D
22. A
23. B
24. D
25. C

TEST 2

DIRECTIONS: Each question or incomplete statement is followed by several suggested answers or completions. Select the one that BEST answers the question or completes the statement. *PRINT THE LETTER OF THE CORRECT ANSWER IN THE SPACE AT THE RIGHT.*

1. The *neighborhood unit* concept does NOT provide for   1.____
   - A. elementary schools
   - B. playgrounds
   - C. local shopping
   - D. industrial development

2. Which of the following areas is LEAST likely to be considered part of social welfare planning?   2.____
   - A. Urban design
   - B. Education
   - C. Health
   - D. Anti-poverty

3. Both the census of business and the census of manufacturing compiled by the U.S. Bureau of the Census are made every _____ years.   3.____
   - A. three
   - B. five
   - C. seven
   - D. ten

4. The MOST frequently used governmental source for topographical maps is the U.S.   4.____
   - A. Department of Agriculture
   - B. Geological Survey
   - C. Department of Housing and Urban Development
   - D. Coast Guard

5. The importance of assessed valuation of land and buildings to a community is to   5.____
   - A. establish school taxes
   - B. establish property taxes
   - C. determine tax exemptions
   - D. determine land uses

6. Of the following countries, the MOST extensive progress in establishing new towns during the 20th century has taken place in   6.____
   - A. the United States
   - B. France
   - C. Italy
   - D. England

7. A street classification system is PRIMARILY used for street   7.____
   - A. naming
   - B. construction
   - C. differentiation
   - D. location

8. The *Greenbelt* towns were a product of the   8.____
   - A. city beautiful movement
   - B. garden city movement
   - C. atomic energy commission
   - D. resettlement administration

9. The apportionment method of population projection is concerned PRIMARILY with

   A. migration
   B. natural increase
   C. large geographic areas
   D. birth rate

10. Under ideal conditions, which type of parking arrangement should yield the MOST parking spaces?

    A. Parallel   B. 45°   C. 60°   D. 90°

11. A MAJOR disadvantage of a depressed highway through a built-up area as compared to a highway on grade is its

    A. poor appearance
    B. inadequate width of right-of-way
    C. lack of access
    D. noise generation

12. The customary test made to determine the ability of a soil to drain off liquids, such as those discharged by a cesspool, is known as the _____ test.

    A. percolation
    B. absorption
    C. drainage
    D. sump

13. The Mitchell-Lama Housing Law was originally intended to assist the construction of

    A. low-income housing
    B. middle-income housing
    C. suburban residential projects
    D. housing for mixed racial communities

14. A community will MOST frequently acquire the development rights of existing farm land in order to

    A. protect land values
    B. provide sites for public projects
    C. insure open space
    D. develop a land bank

15. In recent years, local participation in the city planning process has *substantially* increased because of the

    A. establishment of local school boards
    B. high crime rate in the streets
    C. emergence of private citizen organizations
    D. establishment of community planning boards

16. A unique feature of the State Urban Development Corporation when first established was that it

    A. was an autonomous organization
    B. was not required to conform to local zoning regulations
    C. could only build housing when invited by local communities
    D. used only private funds for its projects

17. The concept of *defensible space* has recently emerged to help fight crime in urban areas. The principle of *defensible space* is that public areas should be

    A. completely enclosed
    B. eliminated
    C. placed adjacent to areas of activity
    D. patroled by volunteer citizen groups

17.____

18. Of the following, the MAJOR planning implication of a 3-bedroom dwelling unit as compared to a 1-bedroom dwelling unit is that

    A. the family with the larger dwelling unit has more income
    B. with larger dwelling units there will be fewer municipal services necessary
    C. more children will be enrolled in school
    D. smaller dwelling units are cheaper to build than larger units

18.____

19. A landscaped buffer strip is MOST appropriately placed between which of the following land uses?

    A. Light and heavy manufacturing
    B. Residential and commercial
    C. Commercial and manufacturing
    D. Residential of low density and residential of high density

19.____

20. The employment trend in the city over the past 20 years has shown that

    A. *both* white collar and blue collar jobs have increased
    B. *both* white collar and blue collar jobs have decreased
    C. *only* white collar jobs have decreased
    D. *only* blue collar jobs have decreased

20.____

21. For traffic safety, the BEST angle between two intersecting streets is

    A. 15   B. 30   C. 45   D. 90

21.____

22. In the city, the system used by the tax department to identify property is by

    A. house numbers   B. zoning maps
    C. block and lot numbers   D. the official city map

22.____

23. The name of the report by which the U.S. Environmental Protection Agency establishes the effect of a proposed project on the environment is called the

    A. input-output analysis   B. economic base study
    C. ambient air study   D. impact statement

23.____

24. Planners recommend that utility lines be located underground because utility lines built this way are

    A. cheaper to construct
    B. not required to follow street alignments
    C. aesthetically more attractive
    D. more efficient

24.____

25. *Scatter-site* housing means that the housing will be 25._____
   A. located in all use districts
   B. built with large areas of recreation space between buildings
   C. of different heights on each site
   D. built on small, by-passed sites in built-up areas

KEY (CORRECT ANSWERS)

1.	D	11.	C
2.	A	12.	A
3.	B	13.	B
4.	B	14.	C
5.	B	15.	D
6.	D	16.	B
7.	C	17.	C
8.	D	18.	C
9.	C	19.	B
10.	D	20.	D

21. D
22. C
23. D
24. C
25. D

EXAMINATION SECTION
TEST 1

DIRECTIONS: Each question or incomplete statement is followed by several suggested answers or completions. Select the one that BEST answers the question or completes the statement. *PRINT THE LETTER OF THE CORRECT ANSWER IN THE SPACE AT THE RIGHT.*

1. The type of open space plaza built in conjunction with high rise buildings, now encouraged by city zoning laws, was first installed in the city of

    A. Lever House
    B. United Nations Headquarters
    C. Rockefeller Center
    D. Lincoln Center

    1._____

2. Of the following, *open space* in a residential site development is BEST insured by

    A. cluster design
    B. gridiron layout
    C. mixed building types
    D. density zoning

    2._____

3. Of the following statements concerning cast iron fronts built in the 19th century in the city, the one that is CORRECT is that they are

    A. still structurally sound
    B. being condemned for structural reasons
    C. not complex enough for preservation even though basically sound
    D. easily duplicated in the modern town houses.

    3._____

4. Of the following, the BEST example of the use of *eminent domain* is a

    A. planning board's reversal of a contested land use
    B. sale of public land for private development
    C. mayor authorizing the implementation of a zoning change
    D. tract of private land taken by the government for public purposes.

    4._____

5. Of the following measures of central tendency, the value of the variable which occurs MOST frequently is called the

    A. arithmetic mean
    B. harmonic mean
    C. median
    D. mode

    5._____

6. A MAJOR reason that industrial plants have been moving out of the city to the suburbs is that

    A. a cheap labor force is available
    B. union influence is eliminated
    C. plants can expand horizontally
    D. they will be closer to their market area

    6._____

7. The total floor area of a building divided by the lot area is called the

    A. net defensible space
    B. floor-area ratio
    C. rentable ratio
    D. open-space factor

    7._____

33

8. The State Multiple Dwelling Law defines a multiple dwelling as one that has _____ dwelling units.

   A. two or more
   B. three or more
   C. five or more
   D. over ten

9. Most zoning ordinances are NOT concerned with

   A. bulk regulations
   B. setbacks
   C. parking
   D. building materials

10. The site plan included in a set of drawings for a housing project will include all of the following EXCEPT

    A. existing structures
    B. easements and rights of way
    C. a plan of a typical floor
    D. boundary lines and distances

11. *Good* neighborhood planning should provide for

    A. the use of loop roads
    B. the use of cul-de-sacs
    C. a combination of loop roads and cul-de-sacs for ease of auto travel
    D. the separation of pedestrians and vehicles

12. An origin-destination survey is PRIMARILY made by

    A. educational planners
    B. market analysis expert
    C. transportation planners
    D. utility planners

13. Of the following, the concept of linear growth in urban areas refers PRIMARILY to growth of

    A. one type of dwelling only in each specific urban area
    B. the urban area along a major highway
    C. one-industry towns in a specific urban area
    D. urban areas in an orderly plan as opposed to haphazard development

14. In urban areas, it is BEST to locate mass transit facilities

    A. underground
    B. water's edge
    C. along major avenues
    D. so as to inter-connect high rise buildings

15. Of the following, the MAJOR contributing factor to the poor air quality in the city is

    A. smokestack emissions
    B. incinerators
    C. industrial waste
    D. auto exhaust emissions

16. The Municipal Loan Program was established to provide funds for

    A. new one-family housing
    B. low-cost housing in built-up areas
    C. altering and renovating old apartment buildings
    D. local planning boards

17. The towns of Radburn and Reston are *similar* to the extent that each   17.____

    A. has a man-made lake
    B. has a high rise housing building
    C. depends almost entirely on a cul-de-sac road system
    D. has mostly one-and two-story housing.

18. Of the following characteristics, the one MOST applicable to *zoning* is that zoning   18.____

    A. requires a sub-division layout for houses
    B. permits planned unit development in selected cases
    C. represents an attempt by local authorities to legally regulate use of land
    D. requires a typical topographic survey before enactment

19. Zoning laws are generally NOT concerned with   19.____

    A. architectural style   B. building heights
    C. land use   D. population density

20. In an average urban community, the percentage of land *usually* devoted to the street system is MOST NEARLY   20.____

    A. 5%   B. 15%   C. 35%   D. 50%

21. The *railroad flat* obtained its name because it   21.____

    A. had all rooms in a straight line
    B. contained efficiency units
    C. was built with dimensions similar to Pullman train roomettes
    D. was originally built for railroad workers

22. A cul-de-sac is a   22.____

    A. circular driveway   B. dead-end road
    C. highway interchange   D. vehicular turning radius

23. MOST zoning ordinances prescribe minimum setbacks in order to provide   23.____

    A. adequate parking space
    B. maximum fire safety
    C. space for landscaping
    D. sufficient access, light, and air

24. The Critical Path Method   24.____

    A. is a form of scheduling operations against time periods and resources
    B. deals with program evaluation and actual costs
    C. concerns least cost estimating and scheduling
    D. is a tool to assure management that operations will proceed readily

25. According to the Building Code, every habitable room must be provided with natural light from windows. The sum of the areas of these windows must be at least equal to what minimum percentage of floor area of the room?   25.____

    A. 5%   B. 10%   C. 20%   D. 25%

KEY (CORRECT ANSWERS)

1.	C	11.	D
2.	A	12.	C
3.	A	13.	B
4.	D	14.	A
5.	D	15.	D
6.	C	16.	C
7.	B	17.	D
8.	B	18.	C
9.	D	19.	A
10.	C	20.	C

21. A
22. B
23. D
24. A
25. B

TEST 2

DIRECTIONS: Each question or incomplete statement is followed by several suggested answers or completions. Select the one that BEST answers the question or completes the statement. *PRINT THE LETTER OF THE CORRECT ANSWER IN THE SPACE AT THE RIGHT.*

1. *Seed* money as it pertains to a new housing development is intended to   1.____

    A. broaden its scope
    B. restrict and channel the budget of the development
    C. encourage flexibilities and alternatives in the construction of development
    D. get it started

2. Incentive zoning is intended to compensate builders for   2.____

    A. inclusion of special projects in their proposal
    B. increasing the assessed valuation of property
    C. diversifying land use constraints
    D. addition of open space

3. A *performance bond* guarantees that   3.____

    A. a contractor will execute the terms of the contract
    B. the architect will oversee the completion of the contract
    C. the owner will pay the contractor upon the completion of his work
    D. the labor unions will enforce the proper completion of the contract

4. For buildings, the Zoning Resolution controls   4.____

    A. use, types, and bulk
    B. structure, materials, and egress
    C. heating, garbage, and superintendence
    D. landmark preservation, urban esthetics, and pollution

5. Of the following, the one that would contribute MOST toward reducing air pollution in an urban area is   5.____

    A. an increase in the number of parking garages
    B. the reduction of the number of cylinders in automobiles
    C. use of lower octane gasoline in automobiles
    D. an effective rapid transit system

6. PUD design refers to   6.____

    A. high rise housing
    B. housing spaced closely to net more open space
    C. less detached houses, more twinned and row houses
    D. roads around groups of houses

7. The one of the following that is the MOST common characteristic of an *educational park* in the United States is   7.____

    A. vertical high schools in large landscaped areas
    B. buildings for various levels of education in a related complex

C. various coeducational facilities at the high school level
D. high schools related to commerce and industry all on one site

8. An advantage of the *gridiron* system of urban layout is that it

A. is most easily saleable by real estate brokers
B. provides the most air and sunlight
C. is easily adapted by surveyors
D. makes use of normal topography

9. When parking is required in urban areas, the one of the following that is the MOST important benefit of creating this parking underground is

A. the cost of the parking project is reduced
B. air pollution in the area is reduced
C. the land above may be used for other purposes
D. cars are then hidden from sight

10. The MAJOR advantage of the use of the *superblock* is that it

A. improves separation of vehicular and pedestrian circulation
B. lends itself to modular expansion
C. affords space to zone residential from industrial areas
D. lends itself to flexible multi-zoning principles

11. The phrase *public right-of-way* refers to

A. civil rights of individuals
B. an easement
C. a city street
D. a public parking garage

12. A city-approved schedule of long-range construction projects extending over approximately a 6-year period is known as a(n)

A. capital improvement program
B. expense budget
C. master plan
D. flow chart

13. *Urban renewal* is the federal program PRIMARILY concerned with

A. urban design
B. advocate planning
C. construction of new housing
D. construction of new highways

14. As used in city planning, the number of persons per acre is referred to as the

A. density   B. use-ratio
C. space-factor   D. census

15. Of the following, the MOST efficient type of sanitary sewage disposal system is a

    A. cesspool
    B. public sewer
    C. septic tank
    D. storm drain

16. Full ownership of a dwelling unit and common ownership of community facilities is known as a

    A. cooperative
    B. rental unit
    C. condominium
    D. high rise development

17. The number of square feet in one acre of land is

    A. 22,100   B. 40,280   C. 43,560   D. 96,000

18. The MAIN function of a *collector street* is to

    A. conduct traffic from local streets to arterials
    B. provide access to abutting property
    C. provide open space between buildings
    D. carry heavy traffic

19. The *distinguishing* characteristic of a topographic map is its

    A. high and low water lines
    B. representation of terrestrial relief
    C. indications of the different types of soils
    D. illustrations of drainage areas

20. The *input-output* technique for urban economic analysis was originally designed for which one of the following economies?

    A. Municipal   B. National   C. State   D. Regional

21. The *cohort survival model* is one method of determining

    A. population
    B. death rate
    C. migration
    D. birth rate

22. Which one of the following items is DIRECTLY related to an urban land use survey?

    A. The classification system
    B. Physiographic features
    C. Flood area data
    D. The economic base

23. According to the requirements of the zoning ordinance, the basis of granting a variance is MOST often

    A. an economic loss
    B. physical hardship
    C. greater density
    D. change of use

24. Restrictive covenants or deed restrictions are MOST often considered to be

    A. local government regulations
    B. supplementary public controls
    C. subdivision plot requirements
    D. private contracts by property owners.

25. In the U.S. as a whole, when land is to be developed, the determination of street alignments would MOST frequently be made by which one of the following regulations? 25.____

    A. Zoning Ordinances
    B. Subdivision Regulations
    C. Health Department Rules
    D. Highway Department specifications

KEY (CORRECT ANSWERS)

1.	D	11.	C
2.	A	12.	A
3.	A	13.	C
4.	A	14.	A
5.	D	15.	B
6.	B	16.	C
7.	B	17.	C
8.	C	18.	A
9.	C	19.	B
10.	A	20.	B

21. A
22. D
23. B
24. D
25. B

EXAMINATION SECTION
TEST 1

DIRECTIONS: Each question or incomplete statement is followed by several suggested answers or completions. Select the one that BEST answers the question or completes the statement. *PRINT THE LETTER OF THE CORRECT ANSWER IN THE SPACE AT THE RIGHT.*

1. The type of open space plaza built in conjunction with high rise buildings, now encouraged by city zoning laws, was first installed in the city of

    A. Lever House
    B. United Nations Headquarters
    C. Rockefeller Center
    D. Lincoln Center

    1.____

2. Of the following, *open space* in a residential site development is BEST insured by

    A. cluster design
    B. gridiron layout
    C. mixed building types
    D. density zoning

    2.____

3. Of the following statements concerning cast iron fronts built in the 19th century in the city, the one that is CORRECT is that they are

    A. still structurally sound
    B. being condemned for structural reasons
    C. not complex enough for preservation even though basically sound
    D. easily duplicated in the modern town houses.

    3.____

4. Of the following, the BEST example of the use of *eminent domain* is a

    A. planning board's reversal of a contested land use
    B. sale of public land for private development
    C. mayor authorizing the implementation of a zoning change
    D. tract of private land taken by the government for public purposes.

    4.____

5. Of the following measures of central tendency, the value of the variable which occurs MOST frequently is called the

    A. arithmetic mean
    B. harmonic mean
    C. median
    D. mode

    5.____

6. A MAJOR reason that industrial plants have been moving out of the city to the suburbs is that

    A. a cheap labor force is available
    B. union influence is eliminated
    C. plants can expand horizontally
    D. they will be closer to their market area

    6.____

7. The total floor area of a building divided by the lot area is called the

    A. net defensible space
    B. floor-area ratio
    C. rentable ratio
    D. open-space factor

    7.____

41

8. The State Multiple Dwelling Law defines a multiple dwelling as one that has _____ dwelling units.

    A. two or more
    B. three or more
    C. five or more
    D. over ten

9. Most zoning ordinances are NOT concerned with

    A. bulk regulations
    B. setbacks
    C. parking
    D. building materials

10. The site plan included in a set of drawings for a housing project will include all of the following EXCEPT

    A. existing structures
    B. easements and rights of way
    C. a plan of a typical floor
    D. boundary lines and distances

11. *Good* neighborhood planning should provide for

    A. the use of loop roads
    B. the use of cul-de-sacs
    C. a combination of loop roads and cul-de-sacs for ease of auto travel
    D. the separation of pedestrians and vehicles

12. An origin-destination survey is PRIMARILY made by

    A. educational planners
    B. market analysis expert
    C. transportation planners
    D. utility planners

13. Of the following, the concept of linear growth in urban areas refers PRIMARILY to growth of

    A. one type of dwelling only in each specific urban area
    B. the urban area along a major highway
    C. one-industry towns in a specific urban area
    D. urban areas in an orderly plan as opposed to haphazard development

14. In urban areas, it is BEST to locate mass transit facilities

    A. underground
    B. water's edge
    C. along major avenues
    D. so as to inter-connect high rise buildings

15. Of the following, the MAJOR contributing factor to the poor air quality in the city is

    A. smokestack emissions
    B. incinerators
    C. industrial waste
    D. auto exhaust emissions

16. The Municipal Loan Program was established to provide funds for

    A. new one-family housing
    B. low-cost housing in built-up areas
    C. altering and renovating old apartment buildings
    D. local planning boards

17. The towns of Radburn and Reston are *similar* to the extent that each   17.____

    A. has a man-made lake
    B. has a high rise housing building
    C. depends almost entirely on a cul-de-sac road system
    D. has mostly one-and two-story housing.

18. Of the following characteristics, the one MOST applicable to *zoning* is that zoning   18.____

    A. requires a sub-division layout for houses
    B. permits planned unit development in selected cases
    C. represents an attempt by local authorities to legally regulate use of land
    D. requires a typical topographic survey before enactment

19. Zoning laws are generally NOT concerned with   19.____

    A. architectural style   B. building heights
    C. land use   D. population density

20. In an average urban community, the percentage of land *usually* devoted to the street system is MOST NEARLY   20.____

    A. 5%   B. 15%   C. 35%   D. 50%

21. The *railroad flat* obtained its name because it   21.____

    A. had all rooms in a straight line
    B. contained efficiency units
    C. was built with dimensions similar to Pullman train roomettes
    D. was originally built for railroad workers

22. A cul-de-sac is a   22.____

    A. circular driveway   B. dead-end road
    C. highway interchange   D. vehicular turning radius

23. MOST zoning ordinances prescribe minimum setbacks in order to provide   23.____

    A. adequate parking space
    B. maximum fire safety
    C. space for landscaping
    D. sufficient access, light, and air

24. The Critical Path Method   24.____

    A. is a form of scheduling operations against time periods and resources
    B. deals with program evaluation and actual costs
    C. concerns least cost estimating and scheduling
    D. is a tool to assure management that operations will proceed readily

25. According to the Building Code, every habitable room must be provided with natural light from windows. The sum of the areas of these windows must be at least equal to what minimum percentage of floor area of the room?   25.____

    A. 5%   B. 10%   C. 20%   D. 25%

KEY (CORRECT ANSWERS)

1.	C	11.	D
2.	A	12.	C
3.	A	13.	B
4.	D	14.	A
5.	D	15.	D
6.	C	16.	C
7.	B	17.	D
8.	B	18.	C
9.	D	19.	A
10.	C	20.	C

21. A
22. B
23. D
24. A
25. B

TEST 2

DIRECTIONS: Each question or incomplete statement is followed by several suggested answers or completions. Select the one that BEST answers the question or completes the statement. *PRINT THE LETTER OF THE CORRECT ANSWER IN THE SPACE AT THE RIGHT.*

1. *Seed* money as it pertains to a new housing development is intended to   1._____

    A. broaden its scope
    B. restrict and channel the budget of the development
    C. encourage flexibilities and alternatives in the construction of development
    D. get it started

2. Incentive zoning is intended to compensate builders for   2._____

    A. inclusion of special projects in their proposal
    B. increasing the assessed valuation of property
    C. diversifying land use constraints
    D. addition of open space

3. A *performance bond* guarantees that   3._____

    A. a contractor will execute the terms of the contract
    B. the architect will oversee the completion of the contract
    C. the owner will pay the contractor upon the completion of his work
    D. the labor unions will enforce the proper completion of the contract

4. For buildings, the Zoning Resolution controls   4._____

    A. use, types, and bulk
    B. structure, materials, and egress
    C. heating, garbage, and superintendence
    D. landmark preservation, urban esthetics, and pollution

5. Of the following, the one that would contribute MOST toward reducing air pollution in an urban area is   5._____

    A. an increase in the number of parking garages
    B. the reduction of the number of cylinders in automobiles
    C. use of lower octane gasoline in automobiles
    D. an effective rapid transit system

6. PUD design refers to   6._____

    A. high rise housing
    B. housing spaced closely to net more open space
    C. less detached houses, more twinned and row houses
    D. roads around groups of houses

7. The one of the following that is the MOST common characteristic of an *educational park* in the United States is   7._____

    A. vertical high schools in large landscaped areas
    B. buildings for various levels of education in a related complex

C. various coeducational facilities at the high school level
D. high schools related to commerce and industry all on one site

8. An advantage of the *gridiron* system of urban layout is that it

   A. is most easily saleable by real estate brokers
   B. provides the most air and sunlight
   C. is easily adapted by surveyors
   D. makes use of normal topography

8.____

9. When parking is required in urban areas, the one of the following that is the MOST important benefit of creating this parking underground is

   A. the cost of the parking project is reduced
   B. air pollution in the area is reduced
   C. the land above may be used for other purposes
   D. cars are then hidden from sight

9.____

10. The MAJOR advantage of the use of the *superblock* is that it

    A. improves separation of vehicular and pedestrian circulation
    B. lends itself to modular expansion
    C. affords space to zone residential from industrial areas
    D. lends itself to flexible multi-zoning principles

10.____

11. The phrase *public right-of-way* refers to

    A. civil rights of individuals
    B. an easement
    C. a city street
    D. a public parking garage

11.____

12. A city-approved schedule of long-range construction projects extending over approximately a 6-year period is known as a(n)

    A. capital improvement program
    B. expense budget
    C. master plan
    D. flow chart

12.____

13. *Urban renewal* is the federal program PRIMARILY concerned with

    A. urban design
    B. advocate planning
    C. construction of new housing
    D. construction of new highways

13.____

14. As used in city planning, the number of persons per acre is referred to as the

    A. density   B. use-ratio
    C. space-factor   D. census

14.____

15. Of the following, the MOST efficient type of sanitary sewage disposal system is a

   A. cesspool
   B. public sewer
   C. septic tank
   D. storm drain

16. Full ownership of a dwelling unit and common ownership of community facilities is known as a

   A. cooperative
   B. rental unit
   C. condominium
   D. high rise development

17. The number of square feet in one acre of land is

   A. 22,100   B. 40,280   C. 43,560   D. 96,000

18. The MAIN function of a *collector street* is to

   A. conduct traffic from local streets to arterials
   B. provide access to abutting property
   C. provide open space between buildings
   D. carry heavy traffic

19. The *distinguishing* characteristic of a topographic map is its

   A. high and low water lines
   B. representation of terrestrial relief
   C. indications of the different types of soils
   D. illustrations of drainage areas

20. The *input-output* technique for urban economic analysis was originally designed for which one of the following economies?

   A. Municipal   B. National   C. State   D. Regional

21. The *cohort survival model* is one method of determining

   A. population
   B. death rate
   C. migration
   D. birth rate

22. Which one of the following items is DIRECTLY related to an urban land use survey?

   A. The classification system
   B. Physiographic features
   C. Flood area data
   D. The economic base

23. According to the requirements of the zoning ordinance, the basis of granting a variance is MOST often

   A. an economic loss
   B. physical hardship
   C. greater density
   D. change of use

24. Restrictive covenants or deed restrictions are MOST often considered to be

   A. local government regulations
   B. supplementary public controls
   C. subdivision plot requirements
   D. private contracts by property owners.

25. In the U.S. as a whole, when land is to be developed, the determination of street alignments would MOST frequently be made by which one of the following regulations?   25.___
    A. Zoning Ordinances
    B. Subdivision Regulations
    C. Health Department Rules
    D. Highway Department specifications

KEY (CORRECT ANSWERS)

1. D
2. A
3. A
4. A
5. D

6. B
7. B
8. C
9. C
10. A

11. C
12. A
13. C
14. A
15. B

16. C
17. C
18. A
19. B
20. B

21. A
22. D
23. B
24. D
25. B

EXAMINATION SECTION
TEST 1

DIRECTIONS: Each question or incomplete statement is followed by several suggested answers or completions. Select the one that BEST answers the question or completes the Statement. *PRINT THE LETTER OF THE CORRECT ANSWER IN THE SPACE AT THE RIGHT.*

1. City planning should aim at

    A. over-all planning
    B. administrative planning
    C. planning of only physical facilities
    D. planning of resources

    1.____

2. The director of planning of a local planning agency is *usually* responsible to the

    A. planning commission
    B. city council
    C. mayor
    D. city manager

    2.____

3. The official map is subject to change ONLY by the

    A. planning commission
    B. city engineer
    C. legislative body
    D. mayor

    3.____

4. An official map of a city is generally adopted by, and can ONLY be changed by action of the

    A. city engineer
    B. planning board
    C. legislative body
    D. zoning board of appeals

    4.____

5. Zoning regulations are generally administered by the

    A. building department
    B. planning commission
    C. zoning board of appeals
    D. planning director

    5.____

6. Logical extent of area which should be included in basic studies for a comprehensive city plan is

    A. entire residential area
    B. the neighborhood
    C. area bounded by city boundaries
    D. urban region

    6.____

7. The safest angle (in degrees) for the intersection of two local streets is

    A. 45   B. 60   C. 90   D. 120

    7.____

8. The city-beautiful movement is *usually* associated with work of

    A. L'Enfant   B. Burnham   C. Wright   D. Howard

    8.____

9. The garden city movement is *usually* associated with

    A. Adams   B. Moses   C. Dahir   D. Howard

    9.____

10. The power to permit variances to the zoning resolution is *usually* vested in the

   A. City Planning Commission
   B. Building Department
   C. City Council
   D. Board of Standards and Appeals

11. "Multiple Dwelling Law" is a

   A. federal law
   B. state law
   C. municipal ordinance
   D. law to protect landlords and hotels

12. The BEST map to use in planning a street layout for a new development is

   A. topographic   B. planimetric
   C. photo-mosaic   D. hydrographic chart

13. MAXIMUM auto traffic carrying capacity of a city street is attained at approximate speed of _____ M.P.H.

   A. 10-15   B. 15-25   C. 25-40   D. 40-55

14. A decelerating lane would *most likely* be used in conjunction with a

   A. bridge approach
   B. highway exit
   C. sharp curve on a highway
   D. steep grade on a highway

15. Use of curved streets in suburban development is *desirable* because it

   A. increases sight-distance for motorists
   B. makes a lot layout simpler
   C. forces motorists to reduce speed
   D. reduces surveying costs

16. The LEAST important requirement for a fire hydrant is

   A. accessibility   B. artistic design
   C. frost proof   D. mechanical reliability

17. In general, the *highest* tax return per acre of developed land is

   A. business   B. industry
   C. apartments   D. single family homes

18. The percentage of developed land area in a city normally taken up by the street system is about _____ %.

   A. 15   B. 25   C. 35   D. 45

19. The greatest amount of land in Manhattan is used for

   A. residences   B. stores
   C. offices   D. industry

20. The three "Greenbelt" towns in the United States after World War II were built by   20._____
    A. private capital
    B. the F.H.A.
    C. the Resettlement Administration
    D. the Department of Agriculture

KEY (CORRECT ANSWERS)

1.	A	11.	B
2.	A	12.	A
3.	C	13.	B
4.	C	14.	B
5.	A	15.	C
6.	D	16.	B
7.	C	17.	A
8.	B	18.	C
9.	D	19.	A
10.	D	20.	C

TEST 2

DIRECTIONS: Each question consists of a statement. You are to indicate whether the statement is TRUE (T) or FALSE (F). *PRINT THE LETTER OF THE CORRECT ANSWER IN THE SPACE AT THE RIGHT.*

1. In an *ideal plan,* radial express highways should lead to and through the downtown business center of a city. 1.____

2. In an ideal city plan for a large city, there should be circumferential transit lines NOT giving direct service to the central business district. 2.____

3. Modern limited access express highways for mixed traffic may appropriately be estimated, for purposes of adequacy of design, to have a practical capacity of 1200 to 1500 vehicles per lane per hour. 3.____

4. A city that is growing by constant decennial increments of total population would have a *straight-line* population curve when plotted on semi-logarithmic cross-section paper. 4.____

5. An infant mortality rate of 60 per 1000 live births per annum is representative of good health conditions in northeastern cities of the U.S. 5.____

6. A city which has 4 acres of land in use by industry, per 100 total resident population, would be considered highly industrialized. 6.____

7. The federal government, through the Department of Transportation, assists in financing new state highways within and outside corporate limits of cities. 7.____

8. The "riding habit" of Los Angeles would be expected to be *greater than* that of New York because of greater relative extent of use of private automobiles. 8.____

9. Because of lane friction and traffic weaving, a 4-lane one-way express roadway will NOT achieve a greater vehicle discharge per hour than a 3-lane one-way express roadway, all other design features being the same. 9.____

10. It is *good* practice to locate future playgrounds NOT more than one-quarter mile from any part of residential areas to be served. 10.____

11. An efficiently laid-out 18-hole golf course, under average topographic conditions, can be accomodated within 110 acres. 11.____

12. Elementary school sites of at least 5 acres are representative of good practice. 12.____

13. Senior high school sites of 25 to 40 acres are NOT considered extravagant or excessive under modern design standards. 13.____

14. Future school enrollments can be estimated by extrapolation of a curve showing percentage of total population which was enrolled in the school system in past years. 14.____

15. A "neighborhood unit" is a term used to embrace those planned residential area which constitute area of service of 1 junior high school. 15.____

16. "Company housing" is customarily used to describe colonies of dwelling units owned by an industrial corporation and rented individually to its employees. 16.____

17. In a *well-designed* residential subdivision, area of land in streets should NOT exceed 20 per cent of total area. 17.____

18. It is accepted *good* zoning practice to require large parking areas be screened from adjacent residential zones by landscaping. 18.____

19. "Floor area ratio" is quotient of ground floor area of a building divided by area of its lot. 19.____

20. The term "Unrestricted Districts" designates districts for which no use or area regulations or restrictions are provided by present zoning resolutions. 20.____

21. A rectangular block 200' x 810' has an area of about four acres. 21.____

22. Capacity of a highway *increases* directly with the speed. 22.____

23. A truck farm is prohibited in a residential district. 23.____

24. On a street with a crowned pavement, grade may be reduced to 0.0%. 24.____

25. Climate has NO effect on design of combined sewers. 25.____

26. Subgrade of a highway is the *lowest* grade ensuring adequate drainage. 26.____

27. Underdrainage results when inadequate storm sewers are provided. 27.____

28. Plans for bridges over navigable waterways require Army Corps of Engineers approval. 28.____

29. On a street with crossings at grade, the ONLY safety features added by widening a narrow median strip are further separation of opposing lanes of traffic and reduction of headlight glare. 29.____

30. In rural areas, need of sidewalks along highways depends on density of vehicular and pedestrian traffic and design speed of highway. 30.____

31. It is standard practice to design 2-lane highways with minimum sight distance such that overtaking and passing is possible in any section of the highway. 31.____

32. Widening pavements on curves is for *psychological* reasons ONLY. 32.____

33. An advantage of a concrete pavement is its high salvage value. 33.____

34. A *large* part of city planning consists of correction of mistakes. 34.____

35. Distribution of population is *usually* shown on a dot or density map. 35.____

36. A series of density maps showing population distribution at various dates is of NO more value to a city planner than the latest map of series. 36.____

37. In a *free* port, goods may be stored, repacked, manufactured, and reexported WITHOUT customs formalities. 37.____

38. Urban blight is due *solely* to lack of planning in original development. 38.____

39. The Chamber of Commerce of the United States recommends municipalities adopt building codes permitting use of any material or method of construction which meets minimum required standards of performance. 39.____

40. An accepted reliable method of estimating future population of small municipalities (under 10,000), for 5 years forward from the last census, involves extending past trend of birth rates, death rates, annual statistics of new dwelling units constructed, old dwelling units demolished, and average size of family. 40.____

KEY (CORRECT ANSWERS)

1. F	11. T	21. T	31. F
2. T	12. T	22. F	32. F
3. T	13. T	23. F	33. T
4. F	14. F	24. F	34. T
5. F	15. F	25. F	35. T
6. T	16. T	26. F	36. F
7. T	17. T	27. F	37. T
8. F	18. T	28. T	38. F
9. F	19. F	29. F	39. T
10. T	20. F	30. T	40. T

EXAMINATION SECTION
TEST 1

DIRECTIONS: Each question consists of a statement. You are to indicate whether the statement is TRUE (T) or FALSE (F). *PRINT THE LETTER OF THE CORRECT ANSWER IN THE SPACE AT THE RIGHT.*

1. A building erected for rental purposes on a site is an over-improvement, when a less expensive building would result in a larger rate of return on the equity investment. 1.____

2. A "capital project" is any physical betterment or improvement or any preliminary studies or surveys relative thereto. 2.____

3. In planning a civic center, provision should be made (among others) for sites for municipal offices, high school, police and fire headquarters, public market, etc., if existing structures housing these activities need to be replaced. 3.____

4. Neighborhood parks, under accepted recreation standards, should have a minimum area of 1 acre per 1500 population to be served. 4.____

5. As a general principle, playfields are better located in large parks than as a part of high school sites. 5.____

6. Playgrounds for the 6-14 age group need to be spaced closer together than grade school sites. 6.____

7. The provision of intra-block playlots for pre-school age children is an accepted feature of modern subdivision layout. 7.____

8. A densely populated city which has 10 per cent of its total area in parks and playgrounds should be expected to be better provided with outdoor recreation space than an equivalent city with 15 acres of park per 1000 population, assuming equally good geographic distribution of the facilities in both cases. 8.____

9. In selecting a site for a suburban regional shopping center, it is *more important* to secure location adjacent to densely traveled highways than a location served by equivalent highways with a large reserve of traffic capacity. 9.____

10. As a step in estimating future public school enrollments, first grade enrollments of past years should be correlated with number of births six years prior, with quantitative allowance made for number of new dwelling units constructed in the intervening years. 10.____

11. In estimating future public school enrollments, it is good practice to make separate determinations of the number of children per family expected to enter school from: (a) new single family construction and (b) new multi-family dwelling construction. 11.____

12. As a means of relieving urban traffic congestion, the widening of city streets by acquisition of additional rights-of-way is generally *preferable* to construction of new arterial highways on new rights-of-way which require the same capital outlay for real estate. 12.____

13. Discharge capacity of a 60 m.p.h. express highway should be expected to be *greater* than discharge capacity of the same highway with a 40 m.p.h. enforced speed limit. 13.____

14. A progressive traffic light signal system, as compared with a simultaneous system, should be expected to *reduce* the driving speed of motor vehicles but to *increase* their average overall speed for distances in excess of two miles. 14.___

15. An express highway lane, reserved exclusively for modern buses, could carry 24,000 passengers per hour without standees. 15.___

16. The U.S. Department of Transportation may provide federal aid for state highway approaches to toll bridges. 16.___

17. Bypassing of through inter-city traffic will NOT solve street congestion in central business districts, in cities over 1,000,000 population. 17.___

18. In designing highway underpasses for mixed traffic, provision should be made for a vertical clearance of 15 feet. 18.___

19. Provision of public-aided housing projects for the aged is a feature of Dutch housing policy. 19.___

20. Anticipated need for future street widenings in new residential areas can be provided for by requiring building setbacks as a part of municipal subdivision regulations. 20.___

21. If a building has no setbacks or towers, the product of its percentage of lot coverage multiplied by its height in stories will give its "floor area ratio." 21.___

22. A special use (or special exception use), listed in a zoning ordinance as requiring special approval by the zoning board of appeals in a particular district, should ONLY be granted upon showing of proof of exceptional conditions and unnecessary hardship. 22.___

23. Courts have generally upheld a municipal zoning provision requiring a minimum floor area for a single-family house. 23.___

24. Under MOST zoning resolution provisions, site plans for large residential developments (75,000 sq. ft. of site and over) are subject to approval by both city planning commissions and Boards of Standards and Appeals. 24.___

25. A master plan program should be concerned with remote, future rather than current pressing problems. 25.___

26. Master plan studies should NOT be used until the whole plan is complete. 26.___

27. The public should NOT be informed of work being done on the master plan until it is ready for adoption. 27.___

28. Several base maps are required in planning, the scales of which vary with amount of detail a study involves. 28.___

29. A base map should ALWAYS show street names of all streets. 29.___

30. Large open spaces such as parks and cemeteries should *generally* be included on base maps to serve as land marks. 30.___

31. On maps to be reproduced at reduced size, lettering should be large enough to be readable when reduced. 31.___

32. It is NOT important to date a map relating to long-term plans. 32._____

33. The smaller the community, the more accurately population estimates can be made. 33._____

34. Surveys of pre-school age children affords accurate forecasts of public school enrollment. 34._____

35. The center of population is the geographic center of the developed area of a city. 35._____

KEY(CORRECT ANSWER)

1. T
2. F
3. F
4. F
5. F

6. T
7. F
8. F
9. F
10. T

11. T
12. F
13. F
14. T
15. T

16. T
17. T
18. F
19. T
20. T

21. T
22. F
23. T
24. T
25. F

26. F
27. F
28. T
29. F
30. T

31. T
32. F
33. F
34. F
35. F

TEST 2

DIRECTIONS: Each question consists of a statement. You are to indicate whether the statement is TRUE (T) or FALSE (F). *PRINT THE LETTER OF THE CORRECT ANSWER IN THE SPACE AT THE RIGHT.*

1. Bus transportation is *less* efficient than railroads in serving large masses of commuters. 1.____

2. Airports should be located at LEAST 20 miles beyond the developed area of a city. 2.____

3. "El" lines tend to *depreciate* values of property adjacent to them. 3.____

4. Traffic congestion can *usually* be eliminated by parking meters along the curb in central business districts. 4.____

5. A progressive traffic light system can be more readily installed where the blocks are short. 5.____

6. Sample manual counts to supplement automatic counters are *necessary* to determine truck flow. 6.____

7. The cordon count is a series of counts at various points along a highway. 7.____

8. Average day count is sufficient to determine points or area of congestion. 8.____

9. The largest portion of developed area of a self-contained city is used commercially, i.e.: for business and industry. 9.____

10. Land of *highest* value is usually occupied by industry. 10.____

11. Large cemeteries usually have an *adverse* effect on land values and highway transportation. 11.____

12. Strict control of smoke in industrial plants would *eliminate* the necessity for considering prevailing wind direction. 12.____

13. Zoning as now in effect will automatically eliminate the types of existing uses that do NOT belong in a district. 13.____

14. Limitation of building bulk by zoning is BEST attained by placing a maximum height restriction in the ordinance. 14.____

15. An unrestricted district is really an area NOT zoned. 15.____

16. Location of an express subway station has NO effect on land value pattern of a district. 16.____

17. Exclusion of dwellings in a heavy industrial zone is a *desirable* restriction. 17.____

18. All arterial highway borders should be zoned for business. 18.____

19. Increase in number of trucks makes railroad frontage no longer important in industrial location. 19.____

20. Elementary schools should be near centers of neighborhood units. 20.____

21. Diversification of industry is *advisable* particularly in small cities. 21.____

22. Economy in provision of water and sewer mains should result from properly administered zoning. 22.____

23. Building on undeveloped area *increases* storm water runoff. 23.____

24. Cost of installing and maintaining underground conduits for electricity is about the same as for overhead wire and poles. 24.____

25. Overhead electrical and telephone wires are less costly to install and maintain on curved streets than on a rectangular grid. 25.____

26. Sewer and water lines should be installed *before* streets are paved. 26.____

27. Areas should NOT be zoned for multiple family use until sewers are available. 27.____

28. A land value map is for the checking of fairness of assessments. 28.____

29. Character of land and accessibility are 2 *major* factors determining land values of undeveloped land. 29.____

30. A special assessment is added tax due to construction of a building on a lot. 30.____

31. Street trees are *more* appropriate in residential rather than business districts. 31.____

32. Offstreet parking is a *reasonable* zoning requirement for new business structures in outlying areas. 32.____

33. A basic industry of a city manufactures products sold outside the city. 33.____

34. Industrially used property, in general, produces tax revenue to the city in excess of cost of municipal services to such property. 34.____

35. All industry should be encouraged to remain or locate in the central district of a city. 35.____

KEY (CORRECT ANSWERS)

1. T
2. F
3. T
4. F
5. F

6. T
7. F
8. F
9. F
10. F

11. T
12. F
13. F
14. F
15. F

16. F
17. T
18. F
19. F
20. T

21. T
22. T
23. T
24. F
25. F

26. T
27. T
28. F
29. T
30. F

31. T
32. T
33. T
34. T
35. F

EXAMINATION SECTION
TEST 1

DIRECTIONS: Each question consists of a statement. You are to indicate whether the statement is TRUE (T) or FALSE (F). *PRINT THE LETTER OF THE CORRECT ANSWER IN THE SPACE AT THE RIGHT.*

1. A building erected for rental purposes on a site is an over-improvement, when a less expensive building would result in a larger rate of return on the equity investment. 1.____

2. A "capital project" is any physical betterment or improvement or any preliminary studies or surveys relative thereto. 2.____

3. In planning a civic center, provision should be made (among others) for sites for municipal offices, high school, police and fire headquarters, public market, etc., if existing structures housing these activities need to be replaced. 3.____

4. Neighborhood parks, under accepted recreation standards, should have a minimum area of 1 acre per 1500 population to be served. 4.____

5. As a general principle, playfields are better located in large parks than as a part of high school sites. 5.____

6. Playgrounds for the 6-14 age group need to be spaced closer together than grade school sites. 6.____

7. The provision of intra-block playlots for pre-school age children is an accepted feature of modern subdivision layout. 7.____

8. A densely populated city which has 10 per cent of its total area in parks and playgrounds should be expected to be better provided with outdoor recreation space than an equivalent city with 15 acres of park per 1000 population, assuming equally good geographic distribution of the facilities in both cases. 8.____

9. In selecting a site for a suburban regional shopping center, it is *more important* to secure location adjacent to densely traveled highways than a location served by equivalent highways with a large reserve of traffic capacity. 9.____

10. As a step in estimating future public school enrollments, first grade enrollments of past years should be correlated with number of births six years prior, with quantitative allowance made for number of new dwelling units constructed in the intervening years. 10.____

11. In estimating future public school enrollments, it is good practice to make separate determinations of the number of children per family expected to enter school from: (a) new single family construction and (b) new multi-family dwelling construction. 11.____

12. As a means of relieving urban traffic congestion, the widening of city streets by acquisition of additional rights-of-way is generally *preferable* to construction of new arterial highways on new rights-of-way which require the same capital outlay for real estate. 12.____

13. Discharge capacity of a 60 m.p.h. express highway should be expected to be *greater* than discharge capacity of the same highway with a 40 m.p.h. enforced speed limit. 13.____

14. A progressive traffic light signal system, as compared with a simultaneous system, should be expected to *reduce* the driving speed of motor vehicles but to *increase* their average overall speed for distances in excess of two miles.   14.___

15. An express highway lane, reserved exclusively for modern buses, could carry 24,000 passengers per hour without standees.   15.___

16. The U.S. Department of Transportation may provide federal aid for state highway approaches to toll bridges.   16.___

17. Bypassing of through inter-city traffic will NOT solve street congestion in central business districts, in cities over 1,000,000 population.   17.___

18. In designing highway underpasses for mixed traffic, provision should be made for a vertical clearance of 15 feet.   18.___

19. Provision of public-aided housing projects for the aged is a feature of Dutch housing policy.   19.___

20. Anticipated need for future street widenings in new residential areas can be provided for by requiring building setbacks as a part of municipal subdivision regulations.   20.___

21. If a building has no setbacks or towers, the product of its percentage of lot coverage multiplied by its height in stories will give its "floor area ratio."   21.___

22. A special use (or special exception use), listed in a zoning ordinance as requiring special approval by the zoning board of appeals in a particular district, should ONLY be granted upon showing of proof of exceptional conditions and unnecessary hardship.   22.___

23. Courts have generally upheld a municipal zoning provision requiring a minimum floor area for a single-family house.   23.___

24. Under MOST zoning resolution provisions, site plans for large residential developments (75,000 sq. ft. of site and over) are subject to approval by both city planning commissions and Boards of Standards and Appeals.   24.___

25. A master plan program should be concerned with remote, future rather than current pressing problems.   25.___

26. Master plan studies should NOT be used until the whole plan is complete.   26.___

27. The public should NOT be informed of work being done on the master plan until it is ready for adoption.   27.___

28. Several base maps are required in planning, the scales of which vary with amount of detail a study involves.   28.___

29. A base map should ALWAYS show street names of all streets.   29.___

30. Large open spaces such as parks and cemeteries should *generally* be included on base maps to serve as land marks.   30.___

31. On maps to be reproduced at reduced size, lettering should be large enough to be readable when reduced.   31.___

32. It is NOT important to date a map relating to long-term plans. 32.____

33. The smaller the community, the more accurately population estimates can be made. 33.____

34. Surveys of pre-school age children affords accurate forecasts of public school enrollment. 34.____

35. The center of population is the geographic center of the developed area of a city. 35.____

KEY(CORRECT ANSWER)

1.	T	16.	T
2.	F	17.	T
3.	F	18.	F
4.	F	19.	T
5.	F	20.	T
6.	T	21.	T
7.	F	22.	F
8.	F	23.	T
9.	F	24.	T
10.	T	25.	F
11.	T	26.	F
12.	F	27.	F
13.	F	28.	T
14.	T	29.	F
15.	T	30.	T

31. T
32. F
33. F
34. F
35. F

TEST 2

DIRECTIONS: Each question consists of a statement. You are to indicate whether the statement is TRUE (T) or FALSE (F). *PRINT THE LETTER OF THE CORRECT ANSWER IN THE SPACE AT THE RIGHT.*

1. Bus transportation is *less* efficient than railroads in serving large masses of commuters. 1.___

2. Airports should be located at LEAST 20 miles beyond the developed area of a city. 2.___

3. "El" lines tend to *depreciate* values of property adjacent to them. 3.___

4. Traffic congestion can *usually* be eliminated by parking meters along the curb in central business districts. 4.___

5. A progressive traffic light system can be more readily installed where the blocks are short. 5.___

6. Sample manual counts to supplement automatic counters are *necessary* to determine truck flow. 6.___

7. The cordon count is a series of counts at various points along a highway. 7.___

8. Average day count is sufficient to determine points or area of congestion. 8.___

9. The largest portion of developed area of a self-contained city is used commercially, i.e.: for business and industry. 9.___

10. Land of *highest* value is usually occupied by industry. 10.___

11. Large cemeteries usually have an *adverse* effect on land values and highway transportation. 11.___

12. Strict control of smoke in industrial plants would *eliminate* the necessity for considering prevailing wind direction. 12.___

13. Zoning as now in effect will automatically eliminate the types of existing uses that do NOT belong in a district. 13.___

14. Limitation of building bulk by zoning is BEST attained by placing a maximum height restriction in the ordinance. 14.___

15. An unrestricted district is really an area NOT zoned. 15.___

16. Location of an express subway station has NO effect on land value pattern of a district. 16.___

17. Exclusion of dwellings in a heavy industrial zone is a *desirable* restriction. 17.___

18. All arterial highway borders should be zoned for business. 18.___

19. Increase in number of trucks makes railroad frontage no longer important in industrial location. 19.___

20. Elementary schools should be near centers of neighborhood units. 20.___

21. Diversification of industry is *advisable* particularly in small cities. 21.____

22. Economy in provision of water and sewer mains should result from properly administered zoning. 22.____

23. Building on undeveloped area *increases* storm water runoff. 23.____

24. Cost of installing and maintaining underground conduits for electricity is about the same as for overhead wire and poles. 24.____

25. Overhead electrical and telephone wires are less costly to install and maintain on curved streets than on a rectangular grid. 25.____

26. Sewer and water lines should be installed *before* streets are paved. 26.____

27. Areas should NOT be zoned for multiple family use until sewers are available. 27.____

28. A land value map is for the checking of fairness of assessments. 28.____

29. Character of land and accessibility are 2 *major* factors determining land values of undeveloped land. 29.____

30. A special assessment is added tax due to construction of a building on a lot. 30.____

31. Street trees are *more* appropriate in residential rather than business districts. 31.____

32. Offstreet parking is a *reasonable* zoning requirement for new business structures in outlying areas. 32.____

33. A basic industry of a city manufactures products sold outside the city. 33.____

34. Industrially used property, in general, produces tax revenue to the city in excess of cost of municipal services to such property. 34.____

35. All industry should be encouraged to remain or locate in the central district of a city. 35.____

KEY (CORRECT ANSWERS)

1.	T	16.	F
2.	F	17.	T
3.	T	18.	F
4.	F	19.	F
5.	F	20.	T
6.	T	21.	T
7.	F	22.	T
8.	F	23.	T
9.	F	24.	F
10.	F	25.	F
11.	T	26.	T
12.	F	27.	T
13.	F	28.	F
14.	F	29.	T
15.	F	30.	F

31. T
32. T
33. T
34. T
35. F

GRAPHS, MAPS, SKETCHES

EXAMINATION SECTION
TEST 1

DIRECTIONS: Each question or incomplete statement is followed by several suggested answers or completions. Select the one that BEST answers the question or completes the statement. *PRINT THE LETTER OF THE CORRECT ANSWER IN THE SPACE AT THE RIGHT.*

Questions 1-7.

DIRECTIONS: Questions 1 to 7, inclusive, are based on information contained on Chart A.

1. Puerto Ricans were the LARGEST number of people in 1._____

    A. 1975 B. 1973 C. 1979 D. 1971

2. At some time between 1974 and 1975, two groups had the same number of persons. These two groups were 2._____

    A. Puerto Rican and Black
    B. Caucasian and Black
    C. Oriental and Black
    D. Puerto Rican and Caucasian

3. In the same year that the Black population reached its GREATEST peak, the LOWEST number of people residing in Revere were of the following group or groups: 3._____

    A. Puerto Rican and Caucasian
    B. Oriental
    C. Puerto Rican
    D. Puerto Rican and Oriental

4. The group which showed the GREATEST increase in population from 1970 to 1979 is 4._____

    A. Puerto Rican
    B. Caucasian
    C. Oriental
    D. not determinable from the graph

5. In 1977, the Black population was higher by APPROXIMATELY 20% over 5._____

    A. 1972 B. 1976 C. 1974 D. 1978

6. The SMALLEST number of people in 1973 were 6._____

    A. Puerto Rican and Black
    B. Oriental and Black
    C. Puerto Rican and Caucasian
    D. Puerto Rican and Oriental

67

7. The percent increase in population of Puerto Ricans from 1971 to 1978 is *most nearly* 7.____
   A. 34%   B. 18%   C. 62%   D. 80%

CHART A

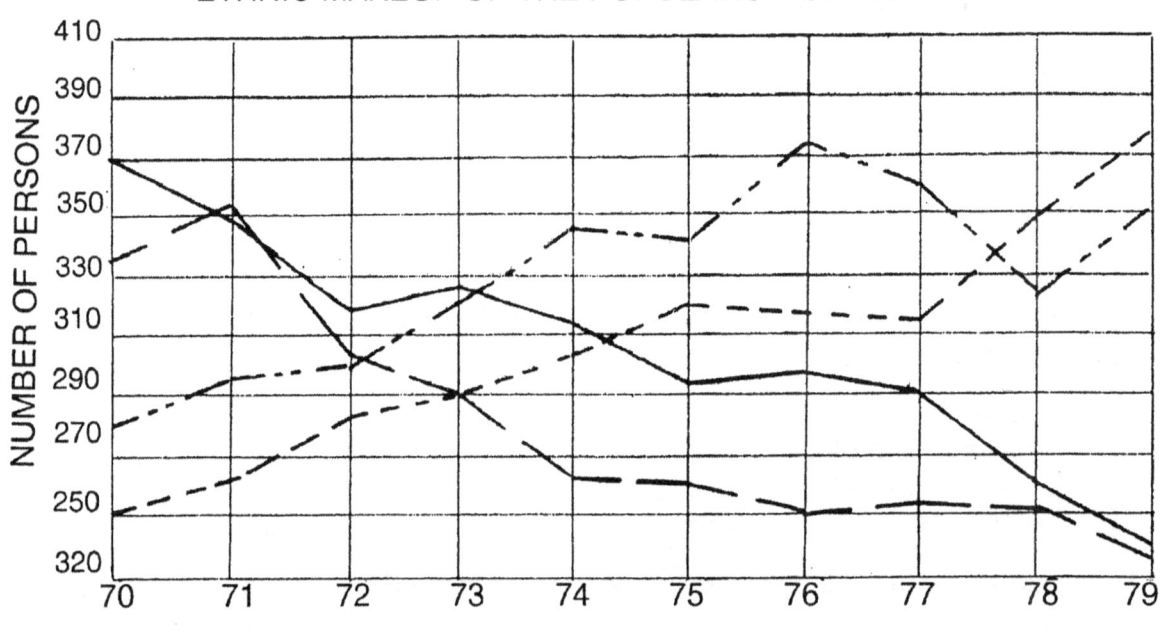

KEY (CORRECT ANSWERS)

1. C
2. D
3. B
4. A
5. A
6. D
7. A

TEST 2

DIRECTIONS: Each question or incomplete statement is followed by several suggested answers or completions. Select the one that BEST answers the question or completes the statement. *PRINT THE LETTER OF THE CORRECT ANSWER IN THE SPACE AT THE RIGHT.*

Questions 1-2.

DIRECTIONS: Questions 1 and 2 are based on information contained on Chart B.

1. The percent of Black middle students attending overcrowded schools in the period 1967 to 1968 is *most nearly*

    A. 34.6   B. 37.6   C. 44.0   D. 47.5

    1._____

2. The percent growth in total school enrollment between 1960-61 and 1967-68 is *most nearly*

    A. 37.6
    B. 45.7
    C. 35.8
    D. cannot be determined from data given

    2._____

CHART B

Summary: School Utilization and Enrollment

PRIMARY SCHOOLS	1960-61	1967-68
NUMBER OF / PERCENT SCHOOLS / UTILIZATION	20/105	20/102
ENROLLMENT/CAPACITY	16685/15842	18204/17813
UTILIZATION: OVER/UNDER	+1942/-1099	+2045/-1654
	NET +843	NET +391
	NO. %	NO. %
WHITE ENROLLMENT	3645 21.8	3146 17.2
NEGRO ENROLLMENT	12691 76.1	14304 78.5
PUERTO RICAN ENROLLMENT	349 2.1	754 4.1

MIDDLE SCHOOLS	1960-61	1967-68
NUMBER OF / PERCENT SCHOOLS / UTILIZATION	3/101	5/96
ENROLLMENT/CAPACITY	4859/4808	7502/7811
UTILIZATION: OVER/UNDER	+235/-174	+276/-585
	NET +61	NET -309
	NO. %	NO. %
WHITE ENROLLMENT	1478 30.4	1717 22.8
NEGRO ENROLLMENT	3279 67.3	5228 69.6
PUERTO RICAN ENROLLMENT	112 2.3	557 7.4

HIGH SCHOOLS	1960-61	1967-68
NUMBER OF / PERCENT SCHOOLS / UTILIZATION	2/78	3/107
ENROLLMENT/CAPACITY	1791/2300	6003/5847
UTILIZATION: OVER/UNDER	+15/-224	+985/-829
	NET -209	NET +156
	NO. %	NO. %
WHITE ENROLLMENT	1106 61.8	3266 54.4
NEGRO ENROLLMENT	650 56.3	2561 42.6
PUERTO RICAN ENROLLMENT	35 2.0	176 2.9

Detail: School Utilization and Enrollment 1967-1968

PRIMARY SCHOOLS	CONSTRUCTION DATES AND TYPE*	GRADES	AVERAGE YRS OVER OR UNDER GRADE	SPECIAL PROGRMS	ENROLLMENT TOTAL	WHITE NO	WHITE %	NEGRO NO	NEGRO %	PUERTO RICAN NO	PUERTO RICAN %	CAPACITY TOTAL	AVAIL- SHORT+	% OF UTIL	OTHER UTIL ROOMS
PS 15	1939	K-5	-.1	T,AS	565	2	.3	523	92.5	40	7.0	669	- 104	84.4	
PS 30	1965	K-5	+1.2	T,AS	1605	854	53.2	748	46.6	3	.1	1099	+ 506	146.0	18 (NOTE M)
PS 34	1931	K-5	+.6	AS	640	345	53.9	259	40.4	36	5.6	702	- 62	91.1	
PS 35	1924,63	K-5	+.7	SS	703	9	1.2	684	97.2	10	1.4	509	+ 194	138.1	6 PORTABLES
PS 36	1928	K-5	+.8	MES,AS	615	61	9.9	544	88.4	10	1.6	419	+ 196	146.7	6 PORTABLES
PS 37	1912,42,64	K-5	-.6	SS,MES	1058	9	.7	994	93.9	55	5.1	869	+ 189	121.7	
PS 40	1914,28,63	K-5	-.2	SS	986	7	.7	949	96.2	30	3.0	856	+ 130	115.1	6 (NOTE N)
PS 45	1936	K-5	-.2	SP	495	10	2.0	482	97.3	3	.1	632	- 137	78.1	4 PORTABLES
PS 48	1922	K-5	-1.2	SS	772	116	15.0	593	76.8	63	8.1	633	+ 41	92.8	1 (NOTE O)
PS 50	1964	K-5	-.5	T,AS	1032	421	40.0	574	54.5	37	5.4	1197	- 145	87.8	
PS 80	1906,30	K-5	-.1		440	375	85.3	21	4.7	44	10.0	378	+ 62	116.4	2 (NOTE P)
PS 92	1925,64	K-5	-.1	SS	1274	489	38.2	647	50.7	138	10.8	1320	- 46	96.5	
PS 116	1923,32	K-5	.0	T	914	2	.3	902	98.6	10	1.0	1067	- 153	85.6	
PS 118	1928,32,64	K-5	-.2	SS	887	28	3.1	832	93.7	27	3.0	1089	- 202	81.4	
PS 123	1928,38	K-5	-1.0	SS	1565	41	2.6	1448	92.5	76	4.8	1103	+ 462	141.8	12 PORTABLES
PS 134	1928,38	K-5	-.3	T	1067	42	3.9	959	89.8	66	6.1	761	+ 306	140.2	
PS 136	1928,37	K-5	-.9	T	987	10	1.0	950	96.2	27	2.7	1301	- 314	75.8	
PS 140	1929,38,63	K-5	-.8	SS	1160	46	3.9	1098	94.6	16	1.3	1241	- 81	93.4	
PS 160	1939	K-5	-1.6	SS	1019	11	1.0	1006	98.7	2	.2	1030	- 11	98.9	
PS 178	1951	K-5	+1.8		400	268	67.0	91	22.7	41	10.2	738	- 336	54.2	1 (NOTE Q)
TOTAL PRIMARY SCHOOLS = 20					18204	3146	17.2	14304	78.5	754	4.1	17813	+ 2045 / - 1654	102.1	

MIDDLE SCHOOLS															
IS 8	1963	6-8	-.5	SS,PI	1562	325	20.8	1124	71.9	113	7.2	1523	+ 39	102.5	
IS 59	1956	6-7	-.1	PI,T,AS	1633	621	38.0	846	51.8	166	10.1	1396	+ 237	116.9	
IS 72	1967	6-8		SS	1396	210	15.0	1171	83.8	15	1.0	1647	- 251	84.7	
IS 142	1930,38	6-8	-1.5		1096	21	1.9	1004	91.6	71	6.4	1333	- 237	82.2	
JS 192	1963	7-9	-.8		1815	540	29.7	1083	59.6	192	10.5	1912	- 97	94.9	
TOTAL MIDDLE SCHOOLS = 5					7502	1717	22.8	5228	69.6	557	7.4	7811	+ 276 / - 585	96.0	

HIGH SCHOOLS															
SPRINGFLD GDNS	1965	9-12	-.3		4277	2758	64.4	1462	34.1	57	1.3	3292	+ 985	129.9	
JAMAICA VOC	1896-C	9-12	-2.9		644	382	59.3	235	36.4	27	4.1	895	- 251	71.9	
W WILSON VOC	1942	9-12	-3.7		1082	126	11.6	864	79.8	92	8.5	1660	- 578	65.1	
TOTAL HIGH SCHOOLS = 3					6003	3266	54.4	2561	42.6	176	2.9	5847	+ 985 / - 829	102.6	

NOTES

1 INCLUDES ENROLLMENT AND CAPACITY AT ANNEX (PS 170) IN QUEENS PLANNING DISTRICT 8
* EXCEPT AS NOTED ALL SCHOOLS ARE OF FIREPROOF CONSTRUCTION
C NOT FIREPROOF
X NOT AVAILABLE

CODE

T: TRANSITIONAL SCHOOL
AS: AFTER SCHOOL STUDY CENTER
SS: SPECIAL SERVICE SCHOOL
MES: MORE EFFECTIVE SCHOOL
SP: SPECIAL PRIMARY SCHOOL
PI: PILOT INTERMEDIATE SCHOOL

NOTES

M IN ROCHDALE VILLAGE
N 4 PORTABLES, 2 IN UNION METHODIST CHURCH
O IN BROOKES MEMORIAL METHODIST CHURCH
P AT 139-35 88TH STREET
Q IN GRACE METHODIST EPISCOPAL CHURCH

KEY (CORRECT ANSWERS)

1. B
2. C

TEST 3

DIRECTIONS: Each question or incomplete statement is followed by several suggested answers or completions. Select the one that BEST answers the question or completes the statement. *PRINT THE LETTER OF THE CORRECT ANSWER IN THE SPACE AT THE RIGHT.*

Questions 1-4.

DIRECTIONS: Questions 1 to 4, inclusive, are based on the information contained on Chart C.

1. What percent of all households in 1960 are Puerto Rican households with incomes of $6,000 or more per year?

   A. 38%   B. 57%   C. 6%   D. 0.6%

   1.____

2. The median income in all households in 1960 is in the range of

   A. $3,000 - $5,999
   B. $6,000 - $9,999
   C. $10,000 - $14,999
   D. cannot be determined from data given

   2.____

3. The total number of white persons living in one or two person households in 1960 is

   A. 13,126   B. 28,884   C. 24,704   D. 46.5

   3.____

4. Which of the following statements is MOST likely to be true?

   A. In 1970, the majority of the population in the above data is white.
   B. The majority of households in 1960 have incomes under $6,000.
   C. There are 8668 people in 1960 in households with incomes under $3,000.
   D. The majority of households in 1960 with incomes under $2,000 are white.

   4.____

2 (#3)

CHART C

Population and Housing Data

Housing Units

	TOTAL	1 ROOM	2 ROOMS	3 ROOMS	4 ROOMS	5 ROOMS	6+ ROOMS
TOTAL HOUSING UNITS - 1960	57611	1484	2492	10491	9074	8409	25661
TOTAL OCCUPIED HOUSING UNITS	56187						
RENTER OCCUPIED - TOTAL	23040						
PUBLIC	1048		44	240	553	199	12
PUBLICLY AIDED	–	–	–	–	–	–	–
OWNER OCCUPIED - TOTAL	33147						
PUBLICLY AIDED	–	–	–	–	–	–	–
PUBLIC HOUSING - 1970							
PUBLIC RENTER	1434	–	44	321	736	300	33
PUBLICLY AIDED RENTER	65	–	–	22	26	17	–
PUBLICLY AIDED OWNER	6075	–	3	2770	2214	568	520

Population Growth

(line chart, x-axis: 1950, 1960, 1970; y-axis: 0 to 250,000)

Income 1960

	PERSONS IN HOUSEHOLD						TOTAL NUMBER OF HOUSEHOLDS
	1	2	3	4	5+		
WHITE HOUSEHOLDS							
UNDER $ 2000	1652	1153	276	143	122		3346
$ 2000 - $ 2999	459	717	176	67	58		1477
$ 3000 - $ 5999	1472	3018	1688	1290	944		8412
$ 6000 - $ 9999	501	3520	2649	2936	1900		10506
$10000 - $14999	75	1378	1255	1069	1148		4925
$15000 AND OVER	17	476	535	637	680		2345
NEGRO AND OTHER NON-WHITE HOUSEHOLDS							
UNDER $ 2000	454	664	366	303	444		2291
$ 2000 - $ 2999	237	453	315	192	280		1477
$ 3000 - $ 5999	587	2368	1721	1804	2313		8793
$ 6000 - $ 9999	98	1735	1984	1650	2465		7932
$10000 - $14999	13	370	547	679	1370		3026
$15000 AND OVER	1	23	82	116	435		656
PUERTO RICAN HOUSEHOLDS							
UNDER $ 2000	9	7	7	11	11		45
$ 2000 - $ 2999	4	2	2	14	12		32
$ 3000 - $ 5999	10	17	45	26	71		169
$ 6000 - $ 9999	1	42	35	30	112		219
$10000 - $14999	1	8	1	21	53		87
$15000 AND OVER	–	–	4	3	19		26
ALL HOUSEHOLDS							
UNDER $ 2000	2155	1826	669	457	577		5682
$ 2000 - $ 2999	700	1170	493	273	350		2986
$ 3000 - $ 5999	2069	5403	3454	2620	1328		16874
$ 6000 - $ 9999	599	5297	4668	3616	4477		18657
$10000 - $14999	92	1756	1857	1769	2567		8041
$15000 AND OVER	17	499	621	756	1134		3027

Ethnic Make-up (in percent)

(bar chart for 1950, 1960, 1970 showing White ○, Black ●, Puerto Rican ●)

Households 1960

% OF ALL HOUSEHOLDS | PERSONS IN HOUSEHOLDS

		1	2	3	4	5	6+
White	56	14	33	21	17	9	7
Black	43	7	23	20	19	13	18
Puerto Rican	1	4	13	17	18	21	27
All Households	100%	12	23	20	17	12	12

KEY (CORRECT ANSWERS)

1. D
2. B
3. C
4. D

TEST 4

DIRECTIONS: Each question or incomplete statement is followed by several suggested answers or completions. Select the one that BEST answers the question or completes the statement. *PRINT THE LETTER OF THE CORRECT ANSWER IN THE SPACE AT THE RIGHT.*

Questions 1-4.

DIRECTIONS: Questions 1 through 4, inclusive, are based on information contained on Chart D.

1. The percentage of households by ethnic make-up in 1960 was *most nearly*

    A. 16% white, 12% Black and other non-white, 16% Puerto Rican, and 56% not reported
    B. 39% white, 26% Black and other non-white, and 35% Puerto Rican
    C. 95% white, 3% Black and 2% Puerto Rican
    D. 99% white, 1% Black and other non-white, and 0% Puerto Rican

    1._____

2. In 1960, the predominant age group was in the age range of

    A. 5-15   B. 25-44   C. 45-64   D. 0-15

    2._____

3. In 1960, the LARGEST singular and discrete income group consisted of households with the following characteristics:

    A. Black and other non-white households of 3 persons with total earnings of between $6,000 and $9,999
    B. White households with 3 persons with total earnings from under $2,000 to $5,999
    C. White households of 2 persons with total earnings between $6,000 and $9,999
    D. White households with total earnings under $2,000

    3._____

4. The percent population increase between 1950 and 1970 was most nearly

    A. 56%   B. 30%   C. 25%   D. 33%

    4._____

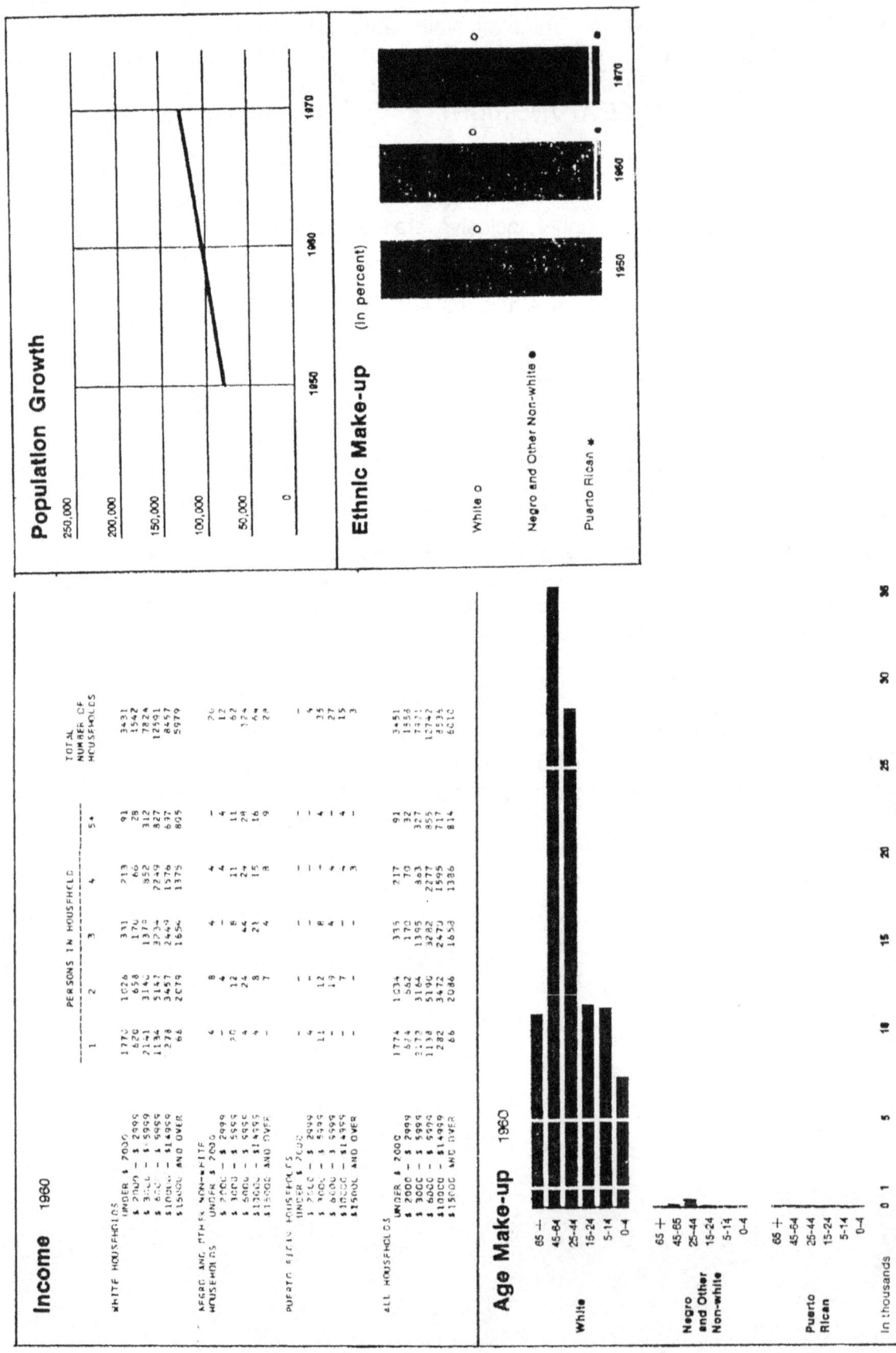

KEY (CORRECT ANSWERS)

1. D
2. C
3. C
4. A

TEST 5

DIRECTIONS: Each question or incomplete statement is followed by several suggested answers or completions. Select the one that BEST answers the question or completes the statement. *PRINT THE LETTER OF THE CORRECT ANSWER IN THE SPACE AT THE RIGHT.*

Questions 1-3.

DIRECTIONS: Questions 1 through 3, inclusive, are based on information contained on Zoning Map E. Zoning Map E is drawn to scale. Candidates are to scale off measurements.

1. One-third of Block A (shaded area) has already been developed as a public housing project. It is proposed that a second development be built on the remainder of the site. The approximate size of the proposed site, in acres, is *most nearly* (43,650 sq.ft. = 1 acre)

    A. 5.9   B. 55   C. 1.8   D. 10.3

    1.____

2. If Site B were developed for housing and 40% of the site was covered by buildings, the amount of open space would be *most nearly* _____ acres.

    A. 2.5   B. 6.3   C. 3.8   D. 2.7

    2.____

3. A new elementary school will have to be built to accommodate the children from the two proposed projects at A and B.
   If the new school must be within 1/2 mile walk of any point in either project, which would be the *most likely* site?

    A. 1   B. 2   C. 3   D. 4

    3.____

ZONING MAP E

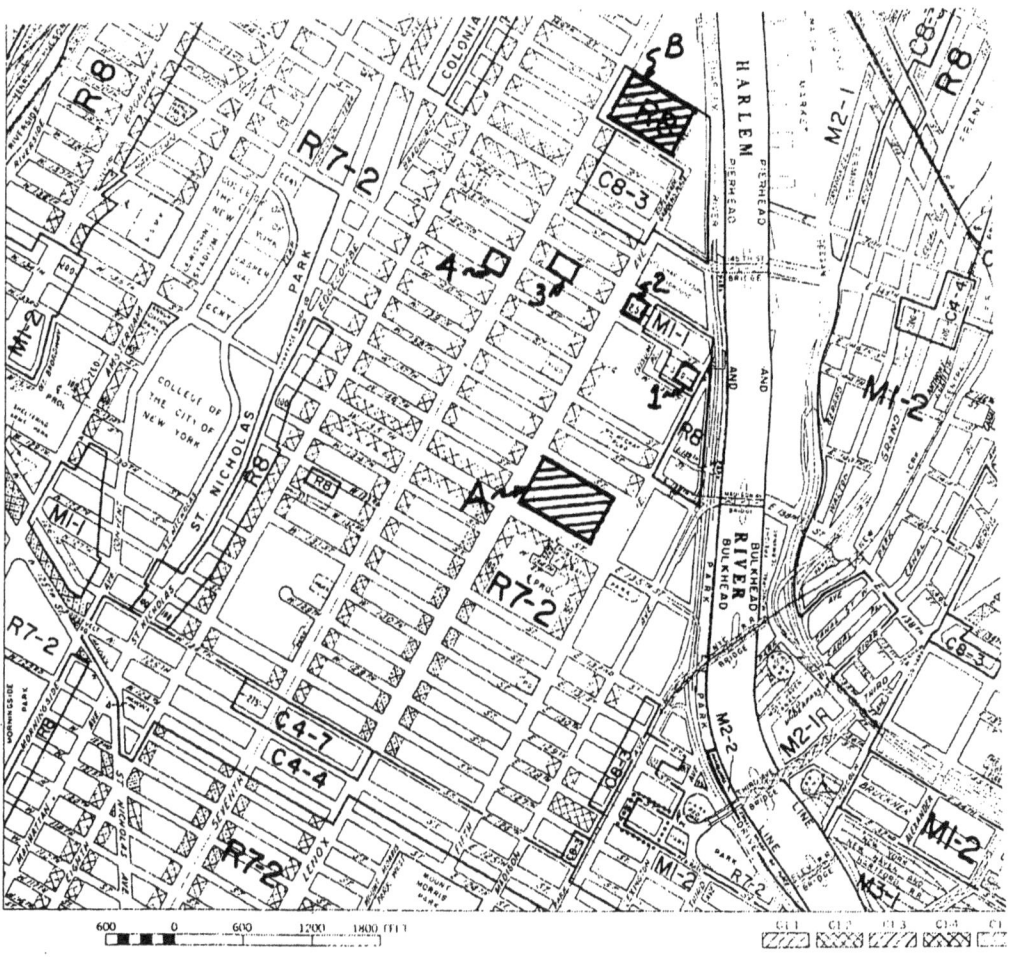

KEY (CORRECT ANSWERS)

1. A
2. C
3. B

TEST 6

DIRECTIONS: Each question or incomplete statement is followed by several suggested answers or completions. Select the one that BEST answers the question or completes the statement. *PRINT THE LETTER OF THE CORRECT ANSWER IN THE SPACE AT THE RIGHT.*

Questions 1-2.

DIRECTIONS: Questions 1 and 2 are to be answered in accordance with the Coast and Geodetic Map F.

1. The difference in elevation between the lowest and highest point of Ewen Park is *most nearly* _____ feet.

   A. 100   B. 25   C. 200   D. 50

2. Given: The scale of the map is as shown.
   The distance between the College of Mt. St. Vincent and Ewen Park is *most nearly* _____ feet.

   A. 2,000   B. 6,000   C. 24,000   D. 12,000

COAST & GEODETIC MAP F

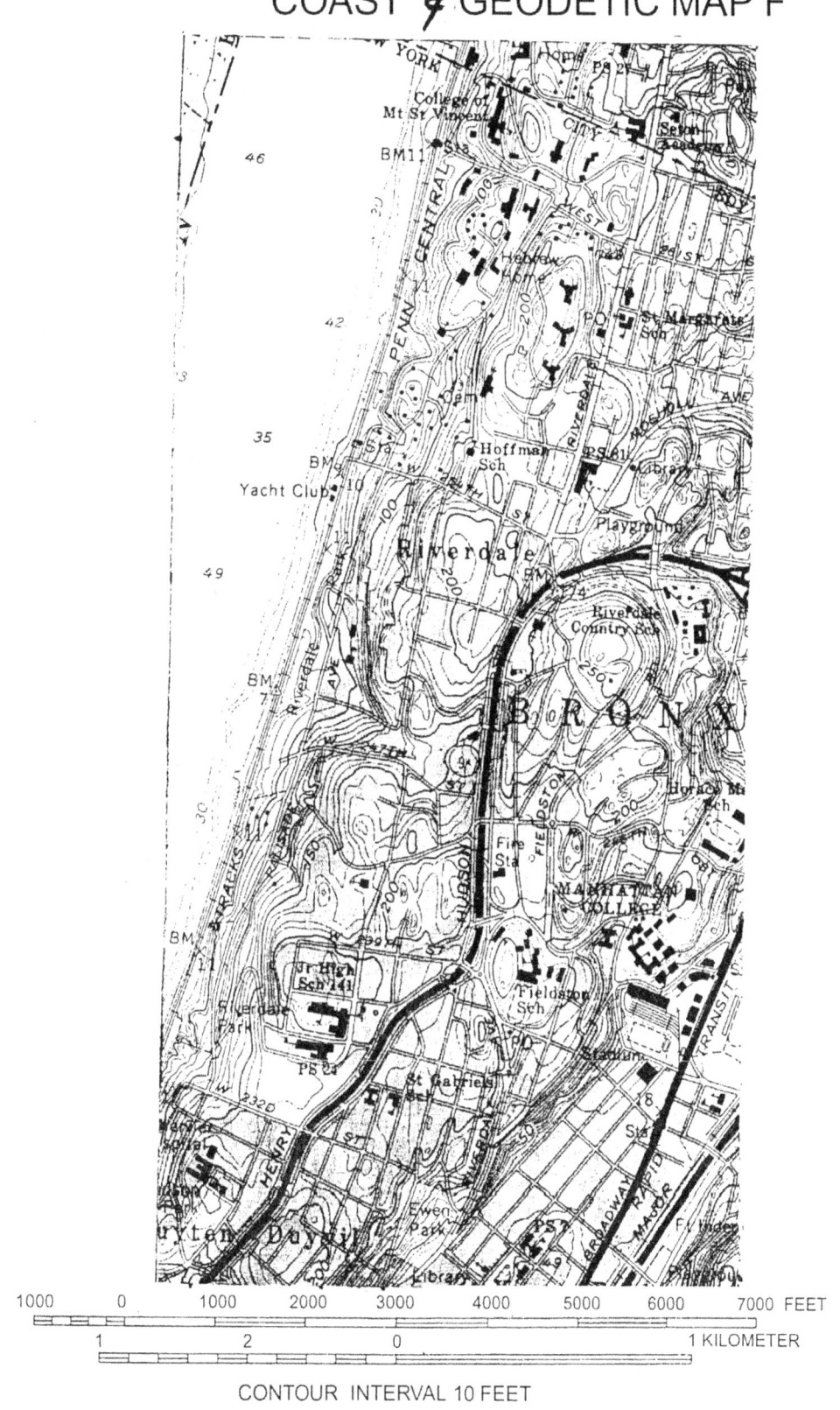

CONTOUR INTERVAL 10 FEET

KEY (CORRECT ANSWERS)

1. A
2. D

TEST 7

DIRECTIONS: Each question or incomplete statement is followed by several suggested answers or completions. Select the one that BEST answers the question or completes the statement. *PRINT THE LETTER OF THE CORRECT ANSWER IN THE SPACE AT THE RIGHT.*

Questions 1-3.

DIRECTIONS: Questions 1 to 3, inclusive, are based on information contained on Sketch G, a birds-eye view of a proposed development.

NOTE: The attached single family homes in the periphery are one-story high and contain 1,000 square feet. They are square buildings.

1. The dimension A of this single family attached home is *most nearly* _____ feet. 1._____
   A. 20   B. 32   C. 50   D. 100

2. The dimension B of the road is *most nearly* _____ feet. 2._____
   A. 25   B. 48   C. 75   D. 100

3. The dimension C of the courtyard is *most nearly* _____ feet. 3._____
   A. 40   B. 85   C. 57   D. 150

83

2 (#7)

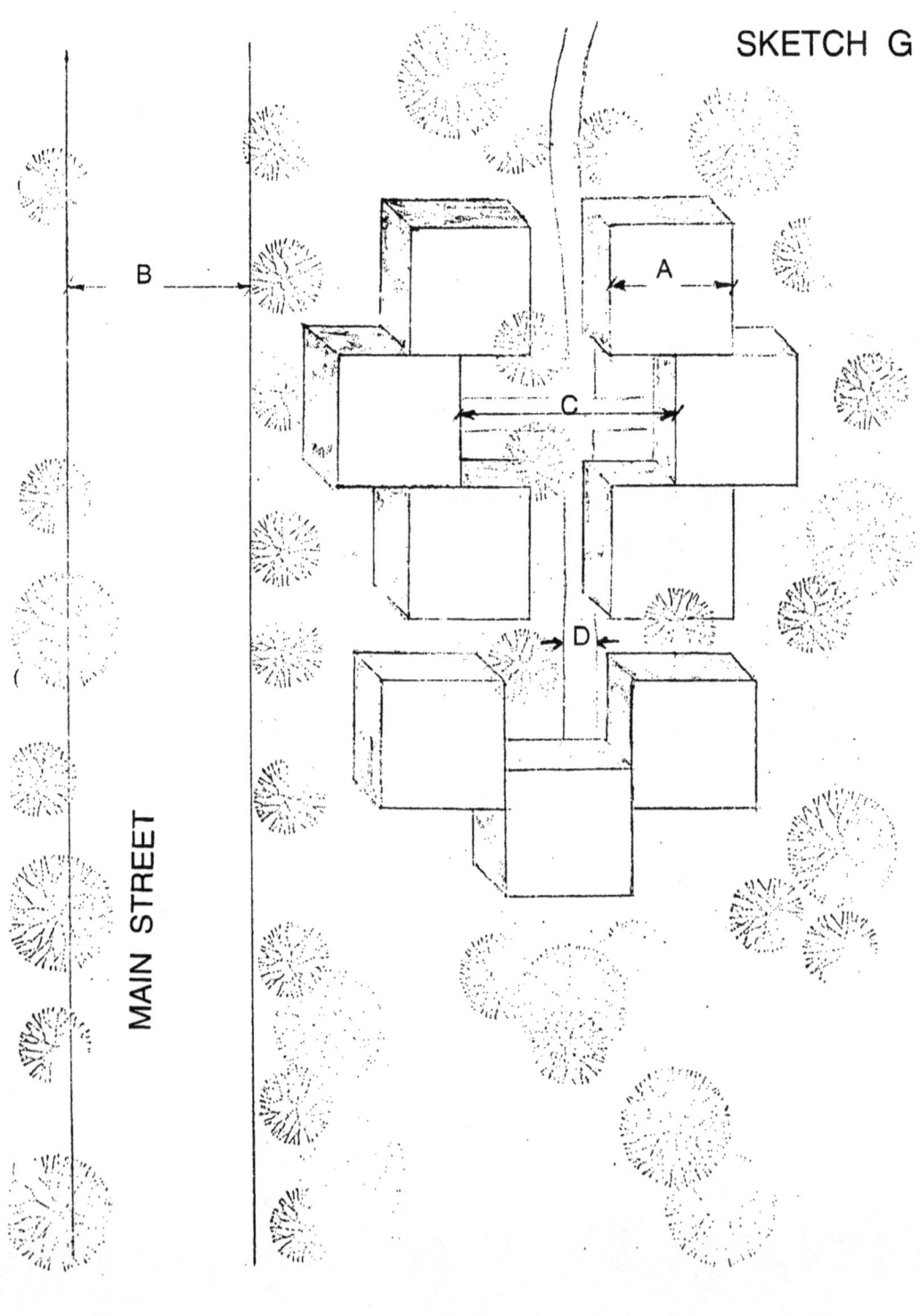

SKETCH G

KEY (CORRECT ANSWERS)

1. B
2. B
3. C

INTERPRETING STATISTICAL DATA GRAPHS, CHARTS AND TABLES
EXAMINATION SECTION
TEST 1

DIRECTIONS: Each question or incomplete statement is followed by several suggested answers or completions. Select the one that BEST answers the question or completes the statement. *PRINT THE LETTER OF THE CORRECT ANSWER IN THE SPACE AT THE RIGHT.*

Questions 1-5.

DIRECTIONS: Questions 1 through 5 are to be answered SOLELY on the basis of the information given in the table below.

AGE COMPOSITION IN THE LABOR FORCE IN CITY A (1990-2000)				
	Age Group	1990	1995	2000
Men	14-24	8,430	10,900	14,340
	25-44	22,200	22,350	26,065
	45+	17,550	19,800	21,970
Women	14-24	4,450	6,915	7,680
	25-44	9,080	10,010	11,550
	45+	7,325	9,470	13,180

1. The GREATEST increase in the number of people in the labor force between 1990 and 1995 occurred among

    A. men between the ages of 14 and 24
    B. men age 45 and over
    C. women between the ages of 14 and 24
    D. women age 45 and over

1.____

2. If the total number of women of all ages in the labor force increases from 2000 to 2005 by the same number as it did from 1995 to 2000, the TOTAL number of women of all ages in the labor force in 2005 will be

    A. 27,425   B. 29,675   C. 37,525   D. 38,425

2.____

3. The total increase in numbers of women in the labor force from 1990 to 1995 differs from the total increase of men in the same years by being _____ than that of men.

    A. 770 less
    B. 670 more
    C. 770 more
    D. 1,670 more

3.____

4. In the year 1990, the proportion of married women in each group was as follows: 1/5 of the women in the 14-24 age group, 1/4 of those in the 25-44 age group, and 2/5 of those 45 and over.
   How many married women were in the labor force in 1990?

    A. 4,625   B. 5,990   C. 6,090   D. 7,910

4.____

5. The 14-24 age group of men in the labor force from 1990 to 2000 increased by APPROXIMATELY 5.___

    A. 40%   B. 65%   C. 70%   D. 75%

KEY (CORRECT ANSWERS)

1. A
2. D
3. B
4. C
5. C

TEST 2

Questions 1-5.

DIRECTIONS: Questions 1 through 5 are to be answered SOLELY on the basis of the information given in the table below.

TYPE OF AREA	STANDARDS FOR RECREATION AREAS			
	ACRES PER 1,000 POPULATION	SIZE OF SITE (ACRES)		RADIUS OF AREAS SERVED (MILES)
		IDEAL	MINIMUM	
Playgrounds	1.5	4	2	0.5
Neighborhood parks	2.0	10	5	0.5
Playfields	1.5	15	10	1.5
Community parks	3.5	100	40	2.0
District parks	2.0	200	100	3.0
Regional parks and reservations	15.0	500-1,000	varies	10.0

1. What is the MINIMUM number of playfields that a community of 15,000 people may contain if the size of each is kept within the limits shown in the table?

    A. 4   B. 10   C. 6   D. 2

2. If, as far as possible, ideal sized playgrounds are built, how many ideal sized playgrounds should a community of 12,000 people contain?

    A. 4   B. 8   C. 1   D. 10

3. APPROXIMATELY how many people can a community park of 200 acres serve?

    A. 120,000   B. 80,000   C. 55,000   D. 20,000

4. If only minimum sized neighborhood parks are built, how many will be required for a population of 20,000?

    A. 5   B. 2   C. 8   D. 12

5. A community of 75,000 persons is evenly distributed over a 5 square mile area. Of the following, the number and size of playgrounds that would BEST satisfy the standards is _____ playgrounds at _____ acres each.

    A. 5;7.5   B. 35;3.5   C. 10;10   D. 50;1.5

KEY (CORRECT ANSWERS)

1. D
2. A
3. C
4. C
5. B

TEST 3

Questions 1-6.

DIRECTIONS: Questions 1 through 6 are to be answered SOLELY on the basis of the following chart.

In a national study of poverty trends, the following data have been assembled for interpretation.

PERSONS BELOW POVERTY LEVEL BY RESIDENCE				
	Number (millions)		Percent	
Item	U.S.	Metropolitan Areas	U.S.	Metropolitan Areas
1999				
Total	38.8	17.0	22.0	15.3
Under 25 years	20.0	8.8	25.3	18.1
65 years	5.5		35.2	26.9
Black	9.9	5.0	55.1	42.8
Other	28.3	11.8	18.1	12.0
2009				
Total	24.3	12.3	12.2	9.5
Under 25 years	12.2		13.2	10.4
65 years & over	4.8	2.3	25.3	20.2
Black	7.2	3.9	32.3	24.4
Other	16.7	8.2	9.5	7.3

1. If no other source of data were available, which of the following groups would you expect to have the HIGHEST rate of poverty?

    A. Others over 65
    B. Others under 65
    C. Blacks over 65
    D. Blacks under 65

2. Between 1999 and 2009, the percentage of poor in the United States who were Black

    A. increased from 25.5% to 29.6%
    B. decreased from 55.1% to 32.3%
    C. decreased from 9.9% to 7.2%
    D. stayed the same

3. The data in the second column of the table indicate that, in metropolitan areas, the number of poor declined by 4.7 million of 36.2% between 1999 and 2009. Yet, the fourth column shows a corresponding decline from 15.3% to 9.5%, or only 5.8%.
   This apparent discrepancy reflects the fact that the

    A. metropolitan areas are growing while the number of poor is contracting
    B. two columns in question are based on different sources of information
    C. difference between two percentages is not the same as the percent change in total numbers
    D. tables have inherent errors and must be carefully checked

4. The percentages in each of the last two columns of the table for 1999 and 2009 don't add up to 100%.
   This is for the reason that

   A. rounding off each entry to the nearest decimal place caused an error in the total such that the total is not equal to 100%
   B. these columns show the percentage of Blacks, aged, etc. who are poor rather than the percentage of poor who are Black, aged, etc.
   C. there was an error in the construction of the table which was not noticed until the table was already in print
   D. there is double counting in the entries in the table; some people are counted more than once

5. Data such as that presented in the table on persons below poverty level are shown to a single decimal place because

   A. data in every table should always be shown to a single decimal place
   B. it is the minimal number of decimal places needed to distinguish among table entries
   C. there was no room for more decimal places in the table without crowding
   D. the more accurately a figure is shown, the better it is for the user

6. In comparing the poverty of the young (under 25 years) with that of the older population (65 years and over) in 1999 and 2009, one could REASONABLY conclude that

   A. more young people than old people were poor but older people had a higher rate of poverty
   B. more older people than young people were poor but young people had a higher rate of poverty
   C. there is a greater degree of poverty among the younger population than among the older people
   D. young people and old people have the same rate of poverty

KEY (CORRECT ANSWERS)

1. C
2. B
3. C
4. B
5. D
6. A

TEST 4

Questions 1-5.

DIRECTIONS: Questions 1 through 5 are to be answered SOLELY on the basis of the table shown below.

POPULATION, URBAN AND RURAL, BY RACE: 1980 TO 2000

In thousands, except percent. An urbanized area comprises at least 1 city of 50,000 inhabitants (central city) plus contiguous closely settled areas (urban fringe). Data for 1980 and 1990 according to urban definition used in the 1990 census; 2000 data according to the 2000 definition.

YEAR AND AREA	TOTAL	WHITE	BLACK AND OTHER	% DISTRIBUTION TOTAL	WHITE	BLACK AND OTHER
1980, total population	151,326	135,150	16,176	100.0	100.0	100.0
Urban	96,847	86,864	9,983	64.0	64.3	61.7
Inside urbanized areas	69,249	61,925	7,324	45.8	45.8	45.3
Central cities	48,377	42,042	6,335	32.0	31.1	39.2
Urban fringe	20,872	19,883	989	13.8	14.7	6.1
Outside urbanized areas	27,598	24,939	2,659	18.2	18.5	16.4
Rural	54,479	48,286	6,193	36.0	35.7	38.3
1990, total population	179,323	158,832	20,491	100.0	100.0	100.0
Urban	125,269	110,428	14,840	69.9	69.5	72.4
Inside urbanized areas	95,848	83,770	12,079	53.5	52.7	58.9
Central cities	57,975	47,627	10,348	32.3	30.0	50.5
Urban fringe	37,873	36,143	1,371	21.1	22.8	8.4
Outside urbanized areas	29,420	26,658	2,762	16.4	16.8	13.5
Rural	54,054	48,403	5,651	30.1	30.5	27.6
2000, total population	203,212	177,749	25,463	100.0	100.0	100.0
Urban	149,325	128,773	20,552	73.5	72.4	80.7
Inside urbanized areas	118,447	100,952	17,495	58.3	56.8	68.7
Central cities	63,922	49,547	14,375	31.5	27.9	56.5
Urban fringe	54,525	51,405	3,120	26.8	28.9	12.3
Outside urbanized areas	30,878	27,822	3,057	15.2	15.7	12.0
Rural	53,887	48,976	4,911	26.5	27.6	19.3

1. The ratio of urban to rural population in 1980 was MOST NEARLY

    A. 3:1   B. 4:1   C. 2:1   D. 1 1/2:1

2. According to the table, the trend of population inside urban areas has been
   A. towards greater concentration
   B. towards less concentration
   C. towards stabilization
   D. erratic

3. Since 1980, the urban fringe white population has substantially increased, while the urban fringe Black and other population has
   A. slightly decreased
   B. greatly decreased
   C. remained the same
   D. increased moderately

4. Over the years, the percentage of the urban white population as compared with the percentage of the total urban population has
   A. remained relatively constant
   B. substantially decreased
   C. substantially increased
   D. varied

5. Select the one of the following which BEST describes the central city white population rate of decrease since 1980 as compared with the central city Black population rate of increase.
   A. The central city white population rate of decrease has been GREATER THAN the central city Black population rate of increase.
   B. The central city white and Black populations have NOT INCREASED to a significant degree.
   C. The central city white population rate of decrease has been EQUAL to the central city Black population rate of increase.
   D. The central city white population rate of decrease has been LESS THAN the central city Black population rate of increase.

KEY (CORRECT ANSWERS)

1. C
2. A
3. D
4. A
5. D

TEST 5

Questions 1-5.

DIRECTIONS: Questions 1 through 4 are to be answered SOLELY on the basis of the information given in the table below.

LIVE BIRTHS, DEATHS, MARRIAGES, AND DIVORCES: 1950-2001

	Number (1,000)					Rate per 1,000 population				
		DEATHS		MAR-	DIVOR		DEATHS		MAR-	DIVOR-
YEAR	BIRTHS	TOTAL	INFANT	RIAGES	-CES	BIRTHS	TOTAL	INFANT	RIAGES	CES
1950	2,777	697	(NA)	948	83	30.1	14.7	(NA)	10.3	0.9
1955	2,965	816	78	1,008	104	29.5	13.2	99.9	10.0	1.0
1960	2,950	1,118	130	1,274	171	27.7	13.0	85.8	12.0	1.6
1965	2,909	1,192	135	1,188	175	25.1	11.7	71.7	10.3	1.5
1970	2,618	1,327	142	1,127	196	21.3	11.3	64.6	9.2	1.6
1975	2,377	1,393	120	1,327	218	18.7	10.9	55.7	10.4	1.7
1980	2,559	1,417	111	1,596	264	19.4	10.8	47.0	12.1	2.0
1985	2,858	1,402	105	1,613	485	20.4	10.6	38.3	12.2	3.5
1990	3,632	1,452	104	1,667	385	24.1	9.6	29.2	11.1	2.6
1995	4,104	1,529	107	1,531	377	25.0	9.3	26.4	9.3	2.3
2000	4,258	1,712	111	1,523	393	23.7	9.5	26.0	8.5	2.2
2001	4,268	1,702	108	1,548	414	23.3	9.3	25.3	8.5	2.3

NA - Not available

1. From 1950 to 2001, the birth rate

    A. approximately doubled
    B. remained stable
    C. been reduced by 25%
    D. had two breaks in its downward progression

2. A comparison of the total population death rate to the infant death rate shows that

    A. the two rates have remained constant
    B. the infant death rate is greater
    C. the total population death rate has decreased at a faster rate
    D. infants had a greater chance to survive in 1955 than in 1990

3. In 1955, about one marriage out of ten ended in divorce.
   In which of the following years would the rate be LESS?

    A. 1995   B. 1975   C. 1960   D. 1950

4. The significance of the decrease in the infant death rate is that 4.____
   A. family size will increase
   B. family size will decrease
   C. family size will not be affected
   D. children will become a smaller percentage of the total population

KEY (CORRECT ANSWERS)

1. C
2. B
3. D
4. C

TEST 6

Questions 1-3.

DIRECTIONS: Questions 1 through 3 are to be answered SOLELY on the basis of the information given in the table below.

The age characteristics of the total population in a certain neighborhood are as follows:

AGE	NUMBER OF PEOPLE
3	2
5	4
12	3
18	3
20	1
21	3
22	4
50	2
56	1
72	2

5. The mean age of the population in the neighborhood described above is MOST NEARLY 5.___

   A. 15 B. 19 C. 23 D. 27

6. The median age of the population in the neighborhood described above is MOST NEARLY 6.___

   A. 15 B. 20 C. 25 D. 30

7. The percentage of the population over age 65 in the neighborhood described above is MOST NEARLY 7.___

   A. 2 B. 4 C. 6 D. 8

KEY (CORRECT ANSWERS)

1. C
2. B
3. D

READING COMPREHENSION
UNDERSTANDING AND INTERPRETING WRITTEN MATERIAL
EXAMINATION SECTION

DIRECTIONS: Each question or incomplete statement is followed by several suggested answers or completions. Select the one that BEST answers the question or completes the statement. *PRINT THE LETTER OF THE CORRECT ANSWER IN THE SPACE AT THE RIGHT.*

TEST 1

Questions 1-2.

DIRECTIONS: Questions 1 and 2 are to be answered SOLELY on the basis of the following passage.

One of the biggest mistakes of government executives with substantial supervisory responsibility is failing to make careful appraisals of performance during employee probationary periods. Many a later headache could have been avoided by prompt and full appraisal during the early months of an employee's assignment. There is not much more to say about this except to emphasize the common prevalence of this oversight and to underscore that for its consequences, which are many and sad, the offending managers have no one to blame but themselves.

1. According to the above passage, probationary periods are
    A. a mistake and should not be used by supervisors with large responsibilities
    B. not used properly by government executives
    C. used only for those with supervisory responsibility
    D. the consequence of management mistakes

1._____

2. The one of the following conclusions that can MOST appropriately be drawn from the above passage is that
    A. management's failure to appraise employees during their probationary period is a common occurrence
    B. there is not much to say about probationary periods because they are unimportant
    C. managers should blame employees for failing to use their probationary periods properly
    D. probationary periods are a headache to most managers

2._____

Questions 3-7.

DIRECTIONS: Questions 3 through 7 are to be answered SOLELY on the basis of the passage preceding each question.

3. Things may not always be what they seem to be. Thus, the wise supervisor should analyze his problems and determine whether there is something there that does not meet the eye. For example, what may seem on the surface to be a personality clash between two subordinates may really be a problem of faulty organization, bad communication, or bad scheduling.
Which one of the following statements BEST supports this passage?
   A. The wise supervisor should avoid personality clashes.
   B. The smart supervisor should figure out what really is going on.
   C. Bad scheduling is the result of faulty organization.
   D. The best supervisor is the one who communicates effectively.

4. Some supervisors, under the pressure of meeting deadlines, become harsh and dictatorial to their subordinates. However, the supervisor most likely to be effective in meeting deadlines is one who absorbs or cushions pressures from above. According to the above passage, if a supervisor wishes to meet deadlines, it is MOST important that he
   A. be informative to his superiors
   B. encourage personal initiative among his subordinates
   C. become harsh and dictatorial to his subordinates
   D. protects his subordinates from pressures from above

5. When giving instructions, a supervisor must always make clear his meaning, leaving no room for misunderstanding. For example, a supervisor who tells a subordinate to do a task *as soon as possible* might legitimately be understood to mean either *it's top priority* or *do it when you can*. Which of the following statements is BEST supported by the above passage?
   A. Subordinates will attempt to avoid work by deliberately distorting instructions.
   B. Instructions should be short, since brief instructions are the clearest.
   C. Less educated subordinates are more likely to honestly misunderstand instructions.
   D. A supervisor should give precise instructions that cannot be misinterpreted.

6. Practical formulas are often suggested to simplify what a supervisor should know and how he should behave, such as the four F's (be firm, fair, friendly, and factual). But such simple formulas are really broad principles, not necessarily specific guides in a real situation. According to the above passage, simple formulas for supervisory behavior
   A. are superior to complicated theories and principles
   B. not always of practical use in actual situations
   C. useful only if they are fair and factual
   D. would be better understood if written in clear language

7. Many management decisions are made far removed from the actual place of operations. Therefore, there is a great need for reliable reports and records and, the larger the organization, the greater is the need for such reports and records. According to the above passage, management decisions made far from the place of operations are
   A. dependent to a great extent on reliable reports and records
   B. sometimes in error because of the great distances involved
   C. generally unreliable because of poor communications
   D. generally more accurate than on-the-scene decisions

Questions 8-9.

DIRECTIONS: Questions 8 and 9 are to be answered SOLELY on the basis of the following passage.

A supervisor who is seeking to influence the behavior of others, whether these others are subordinates, superiors, or colleagues, soon becomes aware of the importance of their attitudes. He may be surprised at some of the attitudes they have and wonder how they can hold some of the views they do - if these views differ from his own. He may be perplexed when others do not change their attitudes even after he has presented facts that obviously should cause them to change.

8. Of the following, the MAIN implication of the above passage is that 8._____
   A. behavior is influenced by factual data
   B. interaction with others is based on factual data
   C. rank and intelligence determine behavior
   D. interpretation of facts is controlled by attitude

9. The one of the following statements MOST directly supported by the above paragraph is: 9._____
   A. A competent supervisor is firm in his views yet retains an open mind
   B. Influencing the behavior of others is usually the most difficult problem in effective supervision
   C. A particular viewpoint may seem unusual to a supervisor holding a contrary opinion
   D. Organizational success depends upon supervisory motivation

Questions 10-13.

DIRECTIONS: Questions 10 through 13 are to be answered SOLELY on the basis of the following passage.

Top public officials, who feel they have tried to improve conditions for their employees, are often bewildered, hurt, or angered when these employees want to do something on their own through union membership. These officials gain little, however, by regarding unionization as an insult or as evidence of failure on their part. The real challenge and opportunity for top officials is to deal constructively with the labor organization which their employees have *duly* chosen to represent them.

10. The author of the above passage MOST likely considers top management to be 10._____
    A. corrupt   B. independent
    C. entrenched   D. paternalistic

11. The above passage points out that certain top public officials are LIKELY to be 11._____
    A. disturbed that employees wish to be unionized
    B. aware of the actual needs of their employees
    C. convinced that labor organizations are ineffectual in gaining benefits
    D. unable to deal constructively with individual employees

12. The tenor of the above passage suggests that
    A. top officials should deal positively with the labor organization
    B. intelligent management practices usually eliminate labor union activities
    C. the labor movement has often opposed enlightened management policies
    D. labor and management have had a long history of disagreement

13. As used in the above passage, the word *duly* means MOST NEARLY
    A. properly or legally   B. forcefully or sincerely
    C. openly or publicly   D. precisely or carefully

Questions 14-17.

DIRECTIONS: Questions 14 through 17 are to be answered SOLELY on the basis of the following passage.

The mental attitude of the employee toward safety is exceedingly important in preventing accidents. All efforts designed to keep safety on the employee's mind and to keep accident prevention a live subject in the office will help substantially in a safety program. Although it may seem strange, it is common for people to be careless. Therefore, safety education is a continuous process.

Safety rules should be explained, and the reasons for their rigid enforcement should be given to employees. Telling employees to be careful or giving similar general safety warnings and slogans is probably of little value. Employees should be informed of basic safety fundamentals. This can be done through staff meetings, informal suggestions to employees, movies, and safety instruction cards. Safety instruction cards provide the employees with specific suggestions about safety and serve as a series of timely reminders helping to keep safety on the minds of employees. Pictures, posters, and cartoon sketches on bulletin boards that are located in areas continually used by employees arouse the employees' interest in safety. It is usually good to supplement this type of safety promotion with intensive individual follow-up.

14. The above passage implies that the LEAST effective of the following safety measures is
    A. rigid enforcement of safety rules
    B. getting employees to think in terms of safety
    C. elimination of unsafe conditions in the office
    D. telling employees to stay alert at all times

15. The reason given by the above passage for maintaining ongoing safety education is that
    A. people are often careless
    B. office tasks are often dangerous
    C. the value of safety slogans increases with repetition
    D. safety rules change frequently

16. Which one of the following safety aids is MOST likely to be preferred by the above passage? 16._____
A
   A. cartoon of a man tripping over a carton and yelling, *Keep aisles clear!*
   B. poster with a large number one and a caption saying, *Safety First*
   C. photograph of a very neatly arranged office
   D. large sign with the word *THINK* in capital letters

17. Of the following, the BEST title for the above passage is 17._____
   A. BASIC SAFETY FUNDAMENTALS
   B. ENFORCING SAFETY AMONG CARELESS EMPLOYEES
   C. ATTITUDES TOWARD SAFETY
   D. MAKING EMPLOYEES AWARE OF SAFETY

Questions 18-21.

DIRECTIONS: Questions 18 through 21 are to be answered SOLELY on the basis of the following passage.

An employee who has been a member of the retirement system continuously for at least two years may thereafter borrow an amount not exceeding forty percent of the amount of his accumulated contributions in the retirement system, provided that he can repay the amount borrowed, with interest, before he reaches age sixty-three by additional deductions of eight percent from his compensation at the time it is paid. The rate of interest payable on such loan shall be three percent higher than the rate of regular interest creditable to his retirement account. The amount borrowed, with interest, shall be repaid in equal installments by deduction from the member's compensation at the time it is paid, but such installments must be equal to at least four percent of the member's compensation.

Each loan shall be insured by the retirement system against the death of the member, as follows: from the twenty-fifth through the fiftieth day after making the loan, thirty percent of the present value of the loan is insured; from the fifty-first through the seventy-fifth day, sixty percent of the present value of the loan is insured; on and after the seventy-sixth day, all of the present value of the loan is insured. Upon the death of the member, the amount of insurance payable shall be credited to his accumulated contributions to the retirement system.

Instead of a loan, any member who cancels his rate of contribution may withdraw from his account, and may restore in any year he chooses, any sum in excess of the maximum in his annuity savings account and due to his account at the end of the calendar year in which he was entitled to cancel his rate of contribution.

18. Based on the information in the above passage, a member may obtain a loan 18._____
   A. in any amount not exceeding forty percent of his accumulated contributions in the system
   B. if he has contributions in excess of the maximum in his annuity savings account
   C. if he will remain a member of the retirement system until age 63
   D. once during his first two years of membership and then at any time thereafter

19. According to the information in the above passage, the interest rate paid by a member who borrows from the retirement system is
    A. 4% of his earnable compensation
    B. 8% of his earnable compensation
    C. lower than the interest rate creditable to his retirement account
    D. higher than the interest rate creditable to his retirement account

19.____

20. Suppose that a member of the retirement system obtained a loan on July 15 of this year and died on October 2 when the present value of her loan was $800. Based on the information in the above passage, this member will have _____ her accumulated contributions to the retirement system.
    A. $480 credited to   B. $480 deducted from
    C. $800 credited to   D. $800 deducted from

20.____

21. Based on the information in the above passage, a member who has excess funds in his retirement account may with- draw funds from the retirement system
    A. if he has cancelled his rate of contribution
    B. if he restores the funds within one year of withdrawal
    C. when he retires
    D. if he leaves city service

21.____

Questions 22-25.

DIRECTIONS: Questions 22 through 25 are to be answered SOLELY on the basis of the following passage.

Upon the death of a member or former member of the retirement system, there shall be paid to his estate, or to the person he had nominated by written designation, his accumulated deductions. In addition, if he is a member who is in city service, there shall be paid a sum consisting of: an amount equal to the compensation he earned while a member during the three months immediately preceding his death, or, if the total amount of years of allowable service exceeds five, there shall be paid an amount equal to the compensation he earned while a member during the six months immediately preceding his death; and the reserve-for-increased-take-home-pay, if any. Payment for the expense of burial, not exceeding two hundred and fifty dollars, may be made to the relative or friend who, in the absence or failure of the designated beneficiary, assumes this responsibility.

Until the first retirement benefit payment has been made, where a member has not selected an option, the member will be considered to be in city service, and the death benefits provided above will be paid instead of the retirement allowance. The member, or upon his death his designated beneficiary, may provide that the actuarial equivalent of the benefit otherwise payable in a lump sum shall be paid in the form of an annuity payable in installments; the amount of such annuity is determined at the time of the member's death on the basis of the age of the beneficiary at that time.

22. Suppose that a member who has applied for retirement benefits without selecting an option dies before receiving any payments.
According to the information in the above passage, this member's beneficiary would be entitled to receive
    A. an annuity based on the member's age at the time of his death
    B. a death benefit only
    C. the member's retirement allowance only
    D. the member's retirement allowance, plus a death benefit payment in a lump sum

22.____

23. According to the information in the above passage, the amount of the benefit payable upon the death of a member is based, in part, on the
    A. length of city service during which the deceased person was a member
    B. number of beneficiaries the deceased member had nominated
    C. percent of the deceased member's deductions for social security
    D. type of retirement plan to which the deceased member belonged

23.____

24. According to the information in the above passage, which one of the following statements concerning the payment of death benefits is CORRECT?
    A. In order for a death benefit to be paid, the deceased member must have previously nominated, in writing, someone to receive the benefit.
    B. Death benefits are paid upon the death of members who are in city service.
    C. A death benefit must be paid in one lump sum.
    D. When a retired person dies, his retirement allowance is replaced by a death benefit payment.

24.____

25. According to the information in the above passage, the amount of annuity payments made to a beneficiary in monthly installments in lieu of a lump sum payment is determined by the
    A. length of member's service at the time of his death
    B. age of the beneficiary at the time of the member's death
    C. member's age at retirement
    D. member's age at the time of his death

25.____

KEY (CORRECT ANSWERS)

1.	B	11.	A	21.	A
2.	A	12.	A	22.	B
3.	B	13.	A	23.	A
4.	D	14.	D	24.	B
5.	D	15.	A	25.	B
6.	B	16.	A		
7.	A	17.	D		
8.	D	18.	A		
9.	C	19.	D		
10.	D	20.	C		

TEST 2

DIRECTIONS: Each question or incomplete statement is followed by several suggested answers or completions. Select the one that BEST answers the question or completes the statement. *PRINT THE LETTER OF THE CORRECT ANSWER IN THE SPACE AT THE RIGHT.*

Questions 1-4.

DIRECTIONS: Questions 1 through 4 are to be answered SOLELY on the basis of the following passage.

Depreciation -- Any reduction from the upper limit of value. An effect caused by deterioration and/or obsolescence. Deterioration is evidenced by wear and tear, decay, dry rot, cracks, encrustations, or structural defects. Obsolescence is divisible into two parts, functional or economic. Functional obsolescence may be due to poor planning, mechanical inadequacy or overadequacy, functional inadequacy or overadequacy due to size, style, or age. It is evidenced by conditions within the property. Economic obsolescence is caused by changes external to the property, such as neighborhood infiltrations of inharmonious groups or property uses, legislation, etc. It is also the actual decline in market value of the improvement to land from the time of purchase to the time of sale.

1. According to the above passage, a form of physical deterioration can be caused by
   A. termite infestation
   B. zoning regulations
   C. inadequate wiring
   D. extra high ceilings

   1._____

2. According to the above passage, a form of economic obsolescence may be caused by
   A. structural defects
   B. poor architectural design
   C. changes in zoning regulations
   D. chemical reactions

   2._____

3. According to the above passage, the statement which BEST explains the meaning of depreciation is that it is a loss in value
   A. caused only by economic obsolescence
   B. resulting from any cause
   C. caused only by wear and tear
   D. resulting from conditions or changes external to the property

   3._____

4. According to the above passage, the lack of air conditioning in warm climates is
   A. a form of physical deterioration
   B. a form of functional obsolescence
   C. a form of economic obsolescence
   D. not a form of depreciation

   4._____

Questions 5-8.

DIRECTIONS: Questions 5 through 8 are to be answered SOLELY on the basis of the following passage.

2 (#2)

In determining the valuation of income-producing property, the capitalization of income is accepted as a proper approach to value. Income-producing property is bought and sold for the purpose of making money. How much an investor would pay would, of course, depend on how much he could earn on his investment. The amount he would earn on his investment is called a return. The amount of return depends on the degree of risk involved.

If one has $100,000 to invest, it can be put in a bank account at perhaps a 5 percent return. In the bank, the money is relatively safe so the return is lower. If the money were invested by purchasing a block of stores in a depressed area, of course, one would not be satisfied with a 5 percent return. This is what the capitalization of income comes down to - the better the return, the higher the risk. This is the approach an experienced real estate investor uses in determining what he would pay for property.

5. According to the above passage, which one of the following investments would an experienced real estate investor with $100,000 MOST likely choose? A(n)
   A. apartment building in a slum area yielding a 6 percent return
   B. office building rented to professionals yielding a 6 percent return
   C. shopping center in a depressed area yielding a 10 percent return
   D. warehouse rented on a long-term lease to a major corporation yielding a 10 percent return

6. According to the above passage, in the capitalization of income, the relationship between the degree of risk and the rate of return GENERALLY is expected to be
   A. indeterminate   B. variable
   C. inverse   D. direct

7. According to the above passage, in purchasing income-producing property, the one of the following which would NOT be a factor influencing an experienced real estate investor is the
   A. socio-economic characteristics of the area in which the property is located
   B. rate of return on investment
   C. original cost of the property
   D. degree of risk involved

8. According to the above passage, the property listed below which would be LEAST likely to be valued by the capitalization of income is a(n)
   A. apartment house with no vacancies
   B. office building rented to 70 percent of capacity
   C. shopping center with several new tenants
   D. vacant lot located next to a factory

Questions 9-12.

DIRECTIONS: Questions 9 through 12 are to be answered SOLELY on the basis of the following passage.

The cost approach is used by assessors mainly in valuing one-family homes and properties of a special nature which are not commonly bought and sold and do not produce an income.

There are three aspects to the cost approach to valuation. The first is the actual cost of construction. Where the property has recently been built, the cost of constructing the property is relevant. It, however, may not be a true test as to its value. The building may have been constructed so as to serve the special needs of the owner. What it costs to construct may not truly reflect its value; it may be worth more or less. If it is income-producing property, the income may be more or less than expected. It may be sold for more or less than it cost to build.

The second aspect is replacement cost and applies to older structures. It involves the construction of a similar type of building with the same purpose. It does not require the use of the same materials or design.

Reproduction cost is the third aspect, and it also applies to older structures. It involves construction with the exact same materials and design. The cost in the two latter aspects is construction at today's prices with an allowance made for depreciation from the day the original building was constructed.

9. According to the above passage, which one of the following is a CORRECT statement concerning the cost approach to valuation?
   A. In determining value by the replacement and reproduction cost methods, an allowance must be made for depreciation from the day the building was originally constructed.
   B. The cost approach method is the best method to apply in valuing an office building.
   C. When a structure has been recently built, its actual cost is the best method of determining its value.
   D. The fact that a structure has been built to meet the special needs of the occupant is a relevant factor in valuation.

10. An assessor, in valuing a ten-year-old apartment house, finds that its original construction cost was $1,200,000. In capitalizing its net income, he realizes a valuation of $800,000. In using the replacement cost method and allowing for depreciation, the assessor arrives at a valuation of $900,000.
   According to the above passage, which one of the following valuations is LEAST acceptable for this apartment house?
   A. $1,200,000 B. $800,000
   C. $900,000   D. $850,000

11. The construction cost of a recently built structure is relevant to value, but may not be a true test of value. According to the above passage, which one of the following statements CORRECTLY explains why this is true?
   A. The builder may not know how to construct economically.
   B. A building can depreciate very quickly.
   C. The building may have been built to satisfy certain unique specifications.
   D. Cost-of-construction is not an accepted method of valuation.

12. According to the above passage, which one of the following statements CORRECTLY defines the essential difference between the replacement cost and reproduction cost aspects of the cost approach?
    A. Replacement cost is used only in assessing older buildings; reproduction cost is used only when the building has been recently constructed.
    B. Reproduction cost does not include any allowance for depreciation; replacement cost allows for depreciation from the date of construction of the original building.
    C. Replacement cost involves construction with the same exact materials; reproduction cost does not require the use of the same materials.
    D. Reproduction cost involves construction with the exact same materials and design; replacement cost does not require the use of the same materials and design.

12._____

Questions 13-18.

DIRECTIONS: Questions 13 through 18 are to be answered SOLELY on the basis of the following passage.

Realty, because of fixity in investment, immobility in location, and necessity for shelter purposes, lends itself readily to economic controls when such are deemed essential to serve social or political ends, or where the interest of health, safety, and morality of community population or the nation at large warrants it. Realty has consistently been recognized as a form of private property which is sufficiently invested with public interest to warrant its control either under the police power of a sovereign state and its branches of government or by direct and statutory legislation enacted within the framework of the governmental constitution.

Whenever war or catastrophe causes a sudden shifting of population or suspension of building operations, or both, an imbalance is brought about in the supply and demand for housing. This imbalance in housing demand and supply creates conditions of insecurity and instability among the tenants who fear indiscriminate eviction or unwarranted upward rental adjustments. It is this background of possible exploitation during times of economic stress and strain that underlies the enactment of emergency rent control legislation.

Although rent control has been in effect in many communities, particularly the larger metropolitan communities, since the end of World War II, the attitude of all levels of government is to view this form of legislation as temporary and to hasten, as far as their power permits, a return to normal relations between landlords and tenants.

13. According to the above passage, the reason that realty can conveniently be subjected to controls is due to
    A. public interest   B. site immobility
    C. population shifts   D. moral considerations

13._____

14. The above passage includes as a justification for the imposition of economic controls all of the following EXCEPT
    A. threats to physical safety
    B. socio-political considerations
    C. dangers to health in the community
    D. requirements of police powers

14._____

15. According to the above passage, a LIKELY cause for a cessation of construction might be a
    A. natural disaster
    B. change in the demand for housing
    C. change in the supply of housing
    D. demographic fluctuations

16. According to the above passage, of the following, a tenant's insecurity would MOST likely result in his fear of
    A. reduction in necessary services
    B. loss in equity
    C. rent increases
    D. condemnation proceedings

17. According to the above passage, indiscriminate evictions by landlords during periods of economic difficulties constitute
    A. unlawful acts
    B. justifiable measures
    C. desirable actions
    D. exploitation of tenants

18. According to the above passage, economic controls of realty have been in effect on a widespread basis since
    A. 1918
    B. 1945
    C. 1953
    D. 1964

Questions 19-22.

DIRECTIONS: Questions 19 through 22 are to be answered SOLELY on the basis of the following passage.

In capitalizing the net income of property to produce a value, certain expenses are permitted to be deducted from gross income. Even though the premises may be fully rented, it is proper to deduct from the gross income an allowance for vacancy. All expenses attributable to the maintenance and upkeep of the premises are deductible. These include heat, light and power, water and sewers, wages or employees and expenses attributable to wages, insurance, repairs and maintenance, supplies and materials, legal and accounting fees, telephone, rental commission, advertising, and so forth. If the premises are furnished, a reserve for the depreciation of personal property is deductible. A capital improvement to the building is not a deductible expense. Real estate taxes should not be deducted as an expense. Instead, taxes should be factored as part of the overall capitalization rate.

It is proper to allow an expense for management of the building even in cases where the owner himself is manager. But payments of interest and principal of the mortgage are not a properly deductible expense. Real property is appraised free and clear of all encumbrances. Otherwise, two identical buildings located next to each other might be valued differently because one has a greater mortgage than the other.

19. According to the above passage, the one of the following which is NOT a proper deductible expense during the year in which the expense is incurred is the cost for
    A. advertising to rent the premises
    B. accounting fees
    C. utilities
    D. putting in central air conditioning

19._____

20. According to the above passage, the one of the following statements concerning deductible expenses which is CORRECT is that
    A. a vacancy allowance is a proper deductible expense even though the premises may be fully rented
    B. real estate taxes are a proper deductible expense
    C. if the owner manages his own property, he cannot charge a management fee as a deductible expense
    D. payments for interest and principal of the mortgage are proper deductible expenses

20._____

21. According to the above passage, two identical adjacent buildings CANNOT receive different valuations because of differences in their
    A. mortgages   B. net income
    C. leases   D. management fees

21._____

22. According to the above passage, an owner of furnished premises may set aside a reserve as a deductible expense for all of the following EXCEPT
    A. refrigerators   B. carpeting
    C. bookcases   D. walls

22._____

Questions 23-25.

DIRECTIONS: Questions 23 through 25 are to be answered SOLELY on the basis of the following passage.

The standard for assessment in the state is contained in Section 306 of the Real Property Tax Law. It states that all real property in each assessing unit shall be assessed at the full value thereof. However, the courts of the state have not required assessors to assess at 100% of full value. Assessments of property for real estate tax purposes at less than full value are not invalid if they are made at a uniform percentage of full value throughout the assessing district. In assessing real property, full value is equivalent to market value.

In determining market value of real property for tax purposes, every element which can reasonably affect value of property ought to be considered, and the main considerations should be given to actual sales of the subject or similar property, cost to produce or reproduce the property, capitalization of income therefrom, and the combination of these factors.

23. According to the above passage, the one of the following statements which is INCORRECT is that all real property in each assessing unit
    A. must be assessed at full value
    B. shall be assessed at full value or at a uniform percentage of full value
    C. may be assessed at 50% of full value
    D. may be assessed at 100% of full value

23._____

24. According to the above passage, the one of the following elements of value which should be given the LEAST consideration in determining market value is
    A. actual or comparable sales
    B. reproduction cost
    C. amount of mortgage
    D. capitalization of income

25. According to the above passage, the basis for the legality of assessing units, making assessments at a uniform percentage of full value rather than at full value is
    A. Section 306 of the Real Property Tax Law
    B. decisions of the state courts
    C. judgments of individual assessors
    D. decisions of municipal executives

KEY (CORRECT ANSWERS)

1.	A	11.	C
2.	C	12.	D
3.	B	13.	B
4.	B	14.	D
5.	D	15.	A
6.	D	16.	C
7.	C	17.	D
8.	D	18.	B
9.	A	19.	D
10.	A	20.	A

21.	A
22.	D
23.	A
24.	C
25.	B

TEST 3

DIRECTIONS: Each question or incomplete statement is followed by several suggested answers or completions. Select the one that BEST answers the question or completes the statement. *PRINT THE LETTER OF THE CORRECT ANSWER IN THE SPACE AT THE RIGHT.*

Questions 1-4.

DIRECTIONS: Questions 1 through 4 are to be answered SOLELY on the basis of the following passage.

Although zoning is a phase of city planning and is concerned with land use control of private property, zoning powers are better known and more generally applied than most city planning powers. Zoning powers predict the formulation of a master plan and even the formation of the planning commission itself. The widespread application of zoning powers is evident from a survey conducted by the International City Managers' Association. As reported in the 2015 MUNICIPAL YEARBOOK, 98 percent of all cities in excess of ten thousand population had enacted comprehensive zoning ordinances governing the utilization of privately owned land. Since 60 percent of all urban land is generally held under private ownership, the impact of zoning laws upon income and value of real property is most significant.

1. According to the above passage, in relation to the powers of city planning, zoning powers are
   A. not as familiar to the general public
   B. formulated subsequent to the establishment of the powers of the planning commission
   C. more general in their application
   D. likely to develop as a result of the community's master plan

1._____

2. According to the above passage, if there are 200 cities in the United States with a population exceeding 10,000 persons, the number of such cities LIKELY to have enacted comprehensive zoning laws is
   A. 190 B. 192
   C. 194 D. 196

2._____

3. According to the above passage, for each 400 acres of urban land, it is LIKELY that the amount of land which would be privately owned would be _____ acres.
   A. 220 B. 240
   C. 260 D. 280

3._____

4. Of the following, the one whose land use is MOST likely to be affected by zoning controls, according to the above passage, is
   A. Sears Department Store
   B. the Port Authority terminal
   C. the New York Public Library at 42nd Street
   D. the Federal Building

4._____

Questions 5-7.

DIRECTIONS: Questions 5 through 7 are to be answered SOLELY on the basis of the following passage.

Apartments located in rehabilitated old law tenement houses are designated as *off-site apartments*. The purpose of such apartments is to provide temporary housing accommodations for the relocation of persons and families living on sites which are to be used for future housing projects who can not otherwise be relocated. A family shall be permitted to continue to occupy an off-site apartment for a period of two years from the date of its admission and shall be required to move out at the termination of such two-year period. However, no proceedings shall be undertaken to remove any tenant now in occupancy of an off-site apartment until after May 9, 2015.

A family shall, however, be required to remove from an off-site apartment prior to the expiration of the periods and date enumerated above if it refuses to accept an available apartment in a public housing project for which it is eligible; or, as a tenant in occupancy, it fails to execute any lease required by management or it fails to comply with other requirements, standard procedures, or rules promulgated by management.

5. A tenant occupying an off-site apartment refuses to renew his lease for one year because he expects to move into a new apartment house within six months. This tenant may
   A. be required to move before his new apartment is ready
   B. be required to move before his new apartment is ready only if his occupancy in the off-site apartment exceeds two years
   C. not be required to move before his new apartment is ready
   D. not be required to move prior to May 9, 2015

5._____

6. According to the above passage, if a family living on a site can be relocated to an apartment in a public housing project, it is
   A. eligible for an off-site apartment near its present dwelling
   B. not eligible for any off-site apartment
   C. eligible for an off-site apartment if it has been living in its present home for at least two years
   D. permitted to continue in occupancy for at least two more years

6._____

7. According to the above passage, a tenant admitted to an off-site apartment on October 1, 2013 is FIRST subject to removal after
   A. October 1, 2015
   B. May 9, 2015
   C. he has been investigated and found to be ineligible for an apartment in the public housing project
   D. he refuses to sign a lease on the apartment or after September 30, 2015, whichever comes first

7._____

Questions 8-14.

DIRECTIONS: Questions 8 through 14 are to be answered SOLELY on the basis of the following passage.

From a nationwide point of view, the need for new housing units during the years immediately ahead will be determined by four major factors. The most important factor is the net change in household formations -- that is, the difference between the number of new households that are formed and the number of existing households that are dissolved, whether by death or other circumstances. During the 2010's, as the children born during the '80's and 90's come of age and marry, the total number of households is expected to increase at a rate of more than 1,000,000 annually. The second factor affecting the need for new housing units is *removals* -- that is, existing units that are demolished, damaged beyond repair, or otherwise removed from the housing supply. A third factor is the number of existing vacancies. To some extent, vacancies can satisfy the housing demand caused by increases in total number of households or by removals, although population shifts that are already underway mean that some areas will have a surfeit of vacancies and other areas will be faced with serious shortages of housing. A final factor, and one that has only recently assumed major importance, is the increasing demand for second homes. These may take any form from a shack in the woods for a city dweller to a pied-a-terre in the city for a suburbanite. Whatever the form, however, it is certain that increasing leisure time, rising amounts of discretionary income, and improvements in transportation are leading more and more Americans to look on a second home not as a rich man's luxury but as the common man's right.

8. The above passage uses the term *housing units* to refer to
    A. residences of all kinds
    B. apartment buildings only
    C. one-family houses only
    D. the total number of families in the United States

9. The above passage uses the word *removals* to mean
    A. the shift of population from one area to another
    B. vacancies that occur when families move
    C. financial losses suffered when a building is damaged or destroyed
    D. former dwellings that are demolished or can no longer be used for housing

10. The expression *pied-a-terre* appears in the next-to-last sentence in the above passage.
    A person who is not familiar with the expression should be able to tell from the way it is used here that it PROBABLY means
    A. a suburban home owned by a commuter
    B. a shack in the woods
    C. a second home that is used from time to time
    D. overnight lodging for a traveler in a strange city

11. Of the factors described in the above passage as having an important influence on the demand for housing, which factor, taken alone, is LEAST likely to encourage the construction of new housing?
    The
    A. net change in household formations
    B. destruction of existing housing
    C. existence of vacancies
    D. use of second homes

12. Based on the above passage, the TOTAL increase in the number of households during the 2010's is expected to be MOST NEARLY
    A. 1,000,000
    B. 10,000,000
    C. 100,000,000
    D. 1,000,000,000

13. Which one of the following conclusions could MOST logically be drawn from the information given in the above passage? 13._____
    A. The population of the United States is increasing at the rate of about 1,000,000 people annually.
    B. There is already a severe housing shortage in all parts of the country.
    C. The need for additional housing units is greater in some parts of the country than in others.
    D. It is still true that only wealthy people can afford to keep up more than one home.

14. Which one of the following conclusions could NOT logically be drawn from the information given in the above passage? 14._____
    A. The need for new housing will be even greater in the 2020's than in the 2010's.
    B. Demolition of existing housing must be taken into account in calculating the need for new housing construction.
    C. Having a second home is more common today than it was in the 1970's.
    D. Part of the housing needs of the 2010's can be met by vacancies.

Questions 15-18.

DIRECTIONS: Questions 15 through 18 are to be answered SOLELY on the basis of the following passage.

A city may expand by growing vertically through the replacement of lower buildings with higher ones; or by filling in open spaces between settled areas; or by extending the existing settled area. When the settled area is expanded, growth may take several forms, the most important forms being concentric circle or ring growth around the central nucleus; axial growth, with prongs or fingerlike extensions moving out along main transportation routes; and suburban growth, with the establishment of islands of settlements before the expansion of the main city area. These types of expansion are characteristic of most large cities. Baltimore was for a long time a good example of ring growth, whereas New York, Chicago, and Detroit illustrate axial and suburban growth.

15. The title that BEST expresses the theme of the above passage is 15._____
    A. FORMS OF CITY EXPANSION
    B. MAJOR METROPOLITAN PROBLEMS
    C. METHODS OF URBAN PLANNING
    D. SUBURBAN GROWTH IN AMERICA

16. The one of the following which is an example of vertical growth is the 16._____
    A. settlement of year-round residents along the upper Hudson River
    B. restoration of former rooming houses to their original brownstone condition
    C. subdivision of large estates into small lot semidetached houses
    D. erection of the Empire State Building in New York City

17. A city that grew as a concentric circle is 17._____
    A. Baltimore   B. New York
    C. Chicago   D. Detroit

18. When the author speaks of axial growth, he refers to a situation where 18._____
    A. expansion is primarily into rural areas until suburbs are thereby created
    B. small towns and villages are consolidated by gradually growing until one large city is created
    C. the direction in which a city expands is determined by the location of major highways
    D. the number of new buildings is greater than the number of old buildings demolished

Questions 19-21.

DIRECTIONS: Questions 19 through 21 are to be answered SOLELY on the basis of the following passage.

Incentive zoning is an affirmative tool that has widespread applications. The Zoning Resolution which became effective in 1998 substantially reduced the amount of floor space that a developer could put up on a given size lot and increased the light and air. In the Trump Building, which was built under the old legislation, the floor space is 27 times the size of the lot. The maximum ratio allowed for buildings now without a special permit is 18.

The 1998 zoning ordinance provided incentives to developers to devote part of the plot to public plazas or arcades. This space is needed to supplement the sidewalks, which in many cases are as narrow as they were when the midtown area was lined with brownstone or brickfront houses.

While the newer zoning has produced plazas, it has not of itself proved to be a sufficient development control. Stretches of Third Avenue and the Avenue of the Americas, for example, have been almost completely redeveloped in the last few years. This massive private investment has produced several fine individual buildings. The total environment produced, however, has been disappointing in a number of respects, and there is nowhere near the amenity that there could have been.

19. According to the above passage, the use of incentive zoning has NOT been entirely successful because it 19._____
    A. has discouraged redevelopment
    B. has encouraged massive private development along Third Avenue
    C. has been ineffective in controlling overall redevelopment
    D. has not significantly increased the number of parks and plazas being built

20. According to the above passage, one might conclude that before the 1998 Zoning Resolution was passed, 20._____
    A. buildings on a given site were required to have greater setbacks
    B. the amount of private investment in development was significantly smaller than it is today
    C. no controls on development existed
    D. the provision of parks and plazas was less frequent

21. In the context of the above passage, the word *amenity* means 21._____
    A. compliance with regulations
    B. correction of undesirable environmental aspects
    C. responsiveness to guidelines and incentives
    D. pleasant or desirable features

Questions 22-24.

DIRECTIONS: Questions 22 through 24 are to be answered SOLELY on the basis of the following passage.

Physical design plays a very significant role in crime rate. Crime rate has been found to increase almost proportionately with building height. The average number of crimes is much greater in higher buildings than in lower ones (equal to or less than six stories). What is most interesting is that in buildings of six stories or less, the project size or total number of units does not make a difference. It seems that although larger projects encourage crime by fostering feelings of anonymity, isolation, irresponsibility, and lack of identity with surroundings, evidence indicates that larger projects encompassed in low buildings seem to offset what we may assume to be factors conducive to high crime rates. High-rise projects not only experience a higher rate of crime within the buildings, but a greater proportion of the crime occurs in the interior public spaces of these buildings as compared with those of the lower buildings. Lower buildings have more limited public space than higher ones. A criminal probably perceives that the interior public areas of buildings are where his victims are most vulnerable and where the possibility of his being seen or apprehended is minimal. Placement of elevators, entrance lobbies, fire stairs, and secondary exits all are factors related to the likelihood of crimes taking place in buildings. The study of all of these elements should bear some weight in the planning of new projects.

22. According to the above passage, which of the following BEST describes the relationship between building size and crime? 22._____
    A. Larger projects lead to a greater crime rate.
    B. Higher buildings tend to increase the crime rate.
    C. The smaller the number of project apartments in low buildings, the higher the crime rate.
    D. Anonymity and isolation serve to lower the crime rate in small buildings.

23. According to the above passage, the likelihood of a criminal attempting a mugging in the interior public portions of a high-rise building is GOOD because 23._____
    A. tenants will be constantly flowing in and out of the area
    B. there is easy access to fire stairs and secondary exits
    C. there is a good chance that no one will see him
    D. tenants may not recognize the victims of crime as their neighbors

24. Which of the following is IMPLIED by the above passage as an explanation for the fact that the crime rate is lower in large low-rise housing projects than in large high-rise projects?
    A. Tenants know each other better and take a greater interest in what happens in the project.
    B. There is more public space where tenants are likely to gather together.
    C. The total number of units in a low-rise project is fewer than the total number of units in a high-rise project.
    D. Elevators in low-rise buildings travel quickly, thus limiting the amount of time in which a criminal can act.

25. The financing of housing represents two distinct forms of costs. One is the actual capital invested, and the other is the interest rate which is charged for the use of capital. In fixing rents, the interest rate which capital is expected to yield plays a very important part. On the basis of this statement, it would be MOST correct to state that
    A. the financing of housing represents two distinct forms of capital investment
    B. reducing the interest rate charged for the use of capital is not as important as economies in construction in achieving lower rentals
    C. in fixing rents, the interest rate is expected to yield capital gains, justifying the investment
    D. the actual capital invested and the interest rate charged for use of this capital are factors in determining housing costs

KEY (CORRECT ANSWERS)

1.	C	11.	C
2.	D	12.	B
3.	B	13.	C
4.	A	14.	A
5.	A	15.	A
6.	B	16.	D
7.	D	17.	A
8.	A	18.	C
9.	D	19.	C
10.	C	20.	D

21.	D
22.	B
23.	C
24.	A
25.	D

EXAMINATION SECTION
TEST 1

DIRECTIONS: Each question or incomplete statement is followed by several suggested answers or completions. Select the one that BEST answers the question or completes the statement. *PRINT THE LETTER OF THE CORRECT ANSWER IN THE SPACE AT THE RIGHT.*

1. When conducting a needs assessment for the purpose of education planning, an agency's FIRST step is to identify or provide
   A. a profile of population characteristics
   B. barriers to participation
   C. existing resources
   D. profiles of competing resources

   1.____

2. Research has demonstrated that of the following, the MOST effective medium for communicating with external publics is(are)
   A. video news releases
   B. television
   C. radio
   D. newspapers

   2.____

3. Basic ideas behind the effort to influence the attitudes and behaviors of a constituency include each of the following EXCEPT the idea that
   A. words, rather than actions or events, are most likely to motivate
   B. demands for action are a usual response
   C. self-interest usually figures heavily into public involvement
   D. the reliability of change programs is difficult to assess

   3.____

4. An agency representative is trying to craft a pithy message to constituents in order to encourage the use of agency program resources.
   Choosing an audience for such messages is easiest when the message
   A. is project- or behavior-based
   B. is combined with other messages
   C. is abstract
   D. has a broad appeal

   4.____

5. Of the following factors, the MOST important to the success of an agency's external education or communication programs is the
   A. amount of resources used to implement them
   B. public's prior experiences with the agency
   C. real value of the program to the public
   D. commitment of the internal audience

   5.____

6. A representative for a state agency is being interviewed by a reporter from a local news network. The representative is being asked to defend a program that is extremely unpopular in certain parts of the municipality.
   When a constituency is known to be opposed to a position, the MOST useful communication strategy is to present

   6.____

A. only the arguments that are consistent with constituents' views
B. only the agency's side of the issue
C. both sides of the argument as clearly as possible
D. both sides of the argument, omitting key information about the opposing position

7. The MOST significant barriers to effective agency community relations include
   I. widespread distrust of communication strategies
   II. the media's "watchdog" stance
   III. public apathy
   IV. statutory opposition

   The CORRECT answer is:
   A. I only   B. I and II   C. II and III   D. III and IV

8. In conducting an education program, many agencies use workshops and seminars in a classroom setting.
   Advantages of classroom-style teaching over other means of educating the public include each of the following, EXCEPT
   A. enabling an instructor to verify learning through testing and interaction with the target audience
   B. enabling hands-on practice and other participatory learning techniques
   C. ability to reach an unlimited number of participants in a given length of time
   D. ability to convey the latest, most up-to-date information

9. The _____ model of community relations is characterized by an attempt to persuade the public to adopt the agency's point of view.
   A. two-way symmetric   B. two-way asymmetric
   C. public information   D. press agency/publicity

10. Important elements of an internal situation analysis include the
    I. list of agency opponents   II. communication audit
    III. updated organizational almanac   IV. stakeholder analysis

    The CORRECT answer is:
    A. I and II   B. I, II, and III   C. II and III   D. I, II, III and IV

11. Government agency information efforts typically involve each of the following objectives, EXCEPT to
    A. implement changes in the policies of government agencies to align with public opinion
    B. communicate the work of agencies
    C. explain agency techniques in a way that invites input from citizens
    D. provide citizen feedback to government administrators

12. Factors that are likely to influence the effectiveness of an educational campaign include the
    I. level of homogeneity among intended participants
    II. number and types of media used
    III. receptivity of the intended participants
    IV. level of specificity in the message or behavior to be taught

    The CORRECT answer is:
    A. I and II
    B. I, II, and III
    C. II and III
    D. I, II, III, and IV

13. An agency representative is writing instructional objectives that will later help to measure the effectiveness of an educational program.
    Which of the following verbs, included in an objective, would be MOST helpful for the purpose of measuring effectiveness?
    A. Know
    B. Identify
    C. Learn
    D. Comprehend

14. A state education agency wants to encourage participation in a program that has just received a boost through new federal legislation. The program is intended to include participants from a wide variety of socioeconomic and other demographic characteristics. The agency wants to launch a broad-based program that will inform virtually every interested party in the state about the program's new circumstances.
    In attempting to deliver this message to such a wide-ranging constituency, the agency's BEST practice would be to
    A. broadcast the same message through as many different media channels as possible
    B. focus on one discrete segment of the public at a time
    C. craft a message whose appeal is as broad as the public itself
    D. let the program's achievements speak for themselves and rely on word-of-mouth

15. Advantages associated with using the World Wide Web as an educational tool include
    I. an appeal to younger generations of the public
    II. visually-oriented, interactive learning
    III. learning that is not confined by space, time, or institutional association
    IV. a variety of methods for verifying use and learning

    The CORRECT answer is:
    A. I only
    B. I and II
    C. I, II, and III
    D. I, II, II, and IV

16. In agencies involved in health care, community relations is a critical function because it
    A. serves as an intermediary between the agency and consumers
    B. generates a clear mission statement for agency goals and priorities
    C. ensures patient privacy while satisfying the media's right to information
    D. helps marketing professionals determine the wants and needs of agency constituents

17. After an extensive campaign to promote its newest program to constituents, an agency learns that most of the audience did not understand the intended message.
MOST likely, the agency has
    A. chosen words that were intended to inform, rather than persuade
    B. not accurately interpreted what the audience really needed to know
    C. overestimated the ability of the audience to receive and process the message
    D. compensated for noise that may have interrupted the message

17._____

18. The necessary elements that lead to conviction and motivation in the minds of participants in an educational or information program include each of the following, EXCEPT the _____ of the message.
    A. acceptability   B. intensity
    C. single-channel appeal   D. pervasiveness

18._____

19. Printed materials are often at the core of educational programs provided by public agencies.
The PRIMARY disadvantage associated with print is that it
    A. does not enable comprehensive treatment of a topic
    B. is generally unreliable in term of assessing results
    C. is often the most expensive medium available
    D. is constrained by time

19._____

20. Traditional thinking on public opinion holds that there is about _____ percent of the public who are pivotal to shifting the balance and momentum of opinion—they are concerned about an issue, but not fanatical, and interested enough to pay attention to a reasoned discussion.
    A. 2   B. 10   C. 33   D. 51

20._____

21. One of the most useful guidelines for influencing attitude change among people is to
    A. invite the target audience to come to you, rather than approaching them
    B. use moral appeals as the primary approach
    C. use concrete images to enable people to see the results of behaviors or indifference
    D. offer tangible rewards to people for changes in behavior

21._____

22. An agency is attempting to evaluate the effectiveness of its educational program. For this purpose, it wants to observe several focus groups discussing the same program.
Which of the following would NOT be a guideline for the use of focus groups?
    A. Focus groups should only include those who have participated in the program.
    B. Be sure to accurately record the discussion.
    C. The same questions should be asked at each focus group meeting.
    D. It is often helpful to have a neutral, non-agency employee facilitate discussions.

22._____

23. Research consistently shows that _____ is the determinant most likely to make a newspaper editor run a news release.
    A. novelty   B. prominence   C. proximity   D. conflict

24. Which of the following is NOT one of the major variables to take into account when considering a population-needs assessment?
    A. State of program development   B. Resources available
    C. Demographics   D. Community attitudes

25. The FIRST step in any communications audit is to
    A. develop a research instrument
    B. determine how the organization currently communicates
    C. hire a contractor
    D. determine which audience to assess

KEY (CORRECT ANSWERS)

1.	A		11.	A
2.	D		12.	D
3.	A		13.	B
4.	A		14.	B
5.	D		15.	C
6.	C		16.	A
7.	D		17.	B
8.	C		18.	C
9.	B		19.	B
10.	C		20.	B

21. C
22. A
23. C
24. C
25. D

TEST 2

DIRECTIONS: Each question or incomplete statement is followed by several suggested answers or completions. Select the one that BEST answers the question or completes the statement. *PRINT THE LETTER OF THE CORRECT ANSWER IN THE SPACE AT THE RIGHT.*

1. A public relations practitioner at an agency has just composed a press release highlighting a program's recent accomplishments and success stories.
   In pitching such releases to print outlets, the practitioner should
   I. e-mail, mail, or send them by messenger
   II. address them to "editor" or "news director"
   III. have an assistant call all media contacts by telephone
   IV. ask reporters or editors how they prefer to receive them

   The CORRECT answer is:
   A. I and II   B. I and IV   C. II, III, and IV   D. III only

   1.____

2. The "output goals" of an educational program are MOST likely to include
   A. specified ratings of services by participants on a standardized scale
   B. observable effects on a given community or clientele
   C. the number of instructional hours provided
   D. the number of participants served

   2.____

3. An agency wants to evaluate satisfaction levels among program participants, and mails out questionnaires to everyone who has been enrolled in the last year.
   The PRIMARY problem associated with this method of evaluative research is that it
   A. poses a significant inconvenience for respondents
   B. is inordinately expensive
   C. does not allow for follow-up or clarification questions
   D. usually involves a low response rate

   3.____

4. A communications audit is an important tool for measuring
   A. the depth of penetration of a particular message or program
   B. the cost of the organization's information campaigns
   C. how key audiences perceive an organization
   D. the commitment of internal stakeholders

   4.____

5. The "ABCs" of written learning objectives include each of the following, EXCEPT
   A. Audience   B. Behavior   C. Conditions   D. Delineation

   5.____

6. When attempting to change the behaviors of constituents, it is important to keep in mind that
   I. most people are skeptical of communications that try to get them to change their behaviors
   II. in most cases, a person selects the media to which he exposes himself
   III. people tend to react defensively to messages or programs that rely on fear as a motivating factor
   IV. programs should aim for the broadest appeal possible in order to include as many participants as possible

   The CORRECT answer is:
   A. I and II   B. I, II and III   C. II and III   D. I, II, III, and IV

7. The "laws" of public opinion include the idea that it is
   A. useful for anticipating emergencies
   B. not sensitive to important events
   C. basically determined by self-interest
   D. sustainable through persistent appeals

8. Which of the following types of evaluations is used to measure public attitudes before and after an information/educational program?
   A. Retrieval study
   B. Copy test
   C. Quota sampling
   D. Benchmark study

9. The PRIMARY source for internal communications is(are) usually
   A. flow charts
   B. meetings
   C. voice mail
   D. printed publications

10. An agency representative is putting together informational materials—brochures and a newsletter—outlining changes in one of the state's biggest benefits programs.
    In assembling print materials as a medium for delivering information to the public, the representative should keep in mind each of the following trends:
    I. For various reasons, the reading capabilities of the public are in general decline
    II. Without tables and graphs to help illustrate the changes, it is unlikely that the message will be delivered effectively
    III. Professionals and career-oriented people are highly receptive to information written in the form of a journal article or empirical study
    IV. People tend to be put off by print materials that use itemized and bulleted (●) lists

    The CORRECT answer is:
    A. I and II   B. I, II and III   C. II and III   D. I, II, III, and IV

11. Which of the following steps in a problem-oriented information campaign would typically be implemented FIRST?
    A. Deciding on tactics
    B. Determining a communications strategy
    C. Evaluating the problem's impact
    D. Developing an organizational strategy

12. A common pitfall in conducting an educational program is to
    A. aim it at the wrong target audience
    B. overfund it
    C. leave it in the hands of people who are in the business of education, rather than those with expertise in the business of the organization
    D. ignore the possibility that some other organization is meeting the same educational need for the target audience

13. The key factors that affect the credibility of an agency's educational program include
    A. organization
    B. scope
    C. sophistication
    D. penetration

14. Research on public opinion consistently demonstrates that it is
    A. easy to move people toward a strong opinion on anything, as long as they are approached directly through their emotions
    B. easier to move people away from an opinion they currently hold than to have them form an opinion about something they have not previously cared about
    C. easy to move people toward a strong opinion on anything, as long as the message appeals to their reason and intellect
    D. difficult to move people toward a strong opinion on anything, no matter what the approach

15. In conducting an education program, many agencies use meetings and conferences to educate an audience about the organization and its programs. Advantages associated with this approach include
    I. a captive audience that is known to be interested in the topic
    II. ample opportunities for verifying learning
    III. cost-efficient meeting space
    IV. the ability to provide information on a wider variety of subjects

    The CORRECT answer is:
    A. I and II   B. I, III and IV   C. II and III   D. I, II, III and IV

16. An agency is attempting to evaluate the effectiveness of its educational programs. For this purpose, it wants to observe several focus groups discussing particular programs.
    For this purpose, a focus group should never number more than _____ participants.
    A. 5   B. 10   C. 15   D. 20

17. A _____ speech is written so that several agency members can deliver it to different audiences with only minor variations.
    A. basic B. printed C. quota D. pattern

18. Which of the following statements about public opinion is generally considered to be FALSE?
    A. Opinion is primarily reactive rather than proactive.
    B. People have more opinions about goals than about the means by which to achieve them.
    C. Facts tend to shift opinion in the accepted direction when opinion is not solidly structured.
    D. Public opinion is based more on information than desire.

19. An agency is trying to promote its educational program.
    As a general rule, the agency should NOT assume that
    A. people will only participate if they perceive an individual benefit
    B. promotions need to be aimed at small, discrete groups
    C. if the program is good, the audience will find out about it
    D. a variety of methods, including advertising, special events, and direct mail, should be considered

20. In planning a successful educational program, probably the first and most important question for an agency to ask is:
    A. What will be the content of the program?
    B. Who will be served by the program?
    C. When is the best time to schedule the program?
    D. Why is the program necessary?

21. Media kits are LEAST likely to contain
    A. fact sheets   B. memoranda
    C. photographs with captions   D. news releases

22. The use of pamphlets and booklets as media for communication with the public often involves the disadvantage that
    A. the messages contained within them are frequently nonspecific
    B. it is difficult to measure their effectiveness in delivering the message
    C. there are few opportunities for people to refer to them
    D. color reproduction is poor

23. The MOST important prerequisite of a good educational program is an
    A. abundance of resources to implement it
    B. individual staff unit formed for the purpose of program delivery
    C. accurate needs assessment
    D. uneducated constituency

24. After an education program has been delivered, an agency conducts a program evaluation to determine whether its objectives have been met.
General rules about how to conduct such an education program valuation include each of the following, EXCEPT that it
   A. must be done immediately after the program has been implemented
   B. should be simple and easy to use
   C. should be designed so that tabulation of responses can take place quickly and inexpensively
   D. should solicit mostly subjective, open-ended responses if the audience was large

25. Using electronic media such as television as means of educating the public is typically recommended ONLY for agencies that
   I. have a fairly simple message to begin with
   II. want to reach the masses, rather than a targeted audience
   III. have substantial financial resources
   IV. accept that they will not be able to measure the results of the campaign with much precision

   The CORRECT answer is:
   A. I and II   B. I, II and III   C. II and IV   D. I, II, III and IV

KEY (CORRECT ANSWERS)

1.	B		11.	C
2.	C		12.	D
3.	D		13.	A
4.	C		14.	D
5.	D		15.	B
6.	B		16.	B
7.	C		17.	D
8.	D		18.	D
9.	D		19.	C
10.	A		20.	D

21.	B
22.	B
23.	C
24.	D
25.	D

EXAMINATION SECTION
TEST 1

DIRECTIONS: Each question or incomplete statement is followed by several suggested answers or completions. Select the one that BEST answers the question or completes the statement. *PRINT THE LETTER OF THE CORRECT ANSWER IN THE SPACE AT THE RIGHT.*

1. Professional staff members in large organizations are sometimes frustrated by a lack of vital work-related information because of the failure of some middle-management supervisors to pass along unrestricted information from top management.
   All of the following are considered to be reasons for such failure to pass along information EXCEPT the supervisors'
   A. belief that information affecting procedures will be ignored unless they are present to supervise their subordinates
   B. fear that specific information will require explanation or justification
   C. inclination to regard the possession of information as a symbol of higher status
   D. tendency to treat information a private property

1.____

2. Increasingly in government, employees' records are being handled by automated data processing systems. However, employees frequently doubt a computer's ability to handle their records properly.
   Which of the following is the BEST way for management to overcome such doubts?
   A. Conduct a public relations campaign to explain the savings certain to result from the use of computers
   B. Use automated data processing equipment made by the firm which has the best repair facilities in the industry
   C. Maintain a clerical force to spot check on the accuracy of the computer's recordkeeping
   D. Establish automated data processing systems that are objective, impartial, and take into account individual factors as far as possible

2.____

3. Some management experts question the usefulness of offering cash to individual employees for their suggestions.
   Which of the following reasons for opposing cash awards is MOST valid?
   A. Emphasis on individual gain deters cooperative effort.
   B. Money spent on evaluating suggestions may outweigh the value of the suggestions.
   C. Awards encourage employees to think about unusual methods of doing work.
   D. Suggestions too technical for ordinary evaluation are usually presented.

3.____

4. The use of outside consultants, rather than regular staff, in studying and recommending improvements in the operations of public agencies has been criticized.
Of the following, the BEST argument in favor of using regular staff is that such staff can better perform the work because they
   A. are more knowledgeable about operations and problems
   B. can more easily be organized into teams consisting of technical specialists
   C. may wish to gain additional professional experience
   D. will provide reports which will be more interesting to the public since they are more experienced

4._____

5. One approach to organizational problem-solving is to have all problem-solving authority centralized at the top of the organization.
However, from the viewpoint of providing maximum service to the public, this practice is UNWISE chiefly because it
   A. reduces the responsibility of the decision-makers
   B. produces delays
   C. reduces internal communications
   D. requires specialists

5._____

6. Research has shown that problem-solving efficiency is optimal when the motivation of the problem-solver is at a moderate rather than an extreme level.
Of the following, probably the CHIEF reason for this is that the problem-solver
   A. will cause confusion among his subordinates when his motivation is too high
   B. must avoid alternate solutions that tend to lead him up blind alleys
   C. can devote his attention to both the immediate problem as well as to other relevant problems in the general area
   D. must feel the need to solve the problem but not so urgently as to direct all his attention to the need and none to the means of solution

6._____

7. Don't be afraid to make mistakes. Many organizations are paralyzed from the fear of making mistakes. As a result, they don't do the things they should; they don't try new and different ideas.
For the effective supervisor, the MOST valid implication of this statement is that
   A. mistakes should not be encouraged, but there are some unavoidable risks in decision-making
   B. mistakes which stem from trying new and different ideas are usually not serious
   C. the possibility of doing things wrong is limited by one's organizational position
   D. the fear of making mistakes will prevent future errors

7._____

8. The duties of an employee under your supervision may be either routine, problem-solving, innovative, or creative.
Which of the following BEST describes duties which are both innovative and creative?

8._____

A. Checking to make sure that work is done properly
B. Applying principles in a practical matter
C. Developing new and better methods of meeting goals
D. Working at two or more jobs at the same time

9. According to modern management theory, a supervisor who uses as little authority as possible and as much as is necessary would be considered to be using a mode that is
    A. autocratic
    B. inappropriate
    C. participative
    D. directive

9.____

10. Delegation involves establishing and maintaining effective working arrangements between a supervisor and the persons who report to him.
Delegation is MOST likely to have taken place when the
    A. entire staff openly discusses common problems in order to reach solutions satisfactory to the supervisor
    B. performance of specified work is entrusted to a capable person, and the expected results are mutually understood
    C. persons assigned to properly accomplish work are carefully evaluated and given a chance to explain shortcomings
    D. supervisor provides specific written instructions in order to prevent anxiety on the part of inexperienced persons

10.____

11. Supervisors often not aware of the effect that their behavior has on their subordinates.
The one of the following training methods which would be BEST for changing such supervisory behavior is _____ training.
    A. essential skills
    B. off-the-job
    C. sensitivity
    D. developmental

11.____

12. A supervisor, in his role as a trainer, may have to decide on the length and frequency of training sessions.
When the material to be taught is new, difficult, and lengthy, the trainer should be guided by the principle that for BEST results in such circumstances, sessions should be
    A. longer, relatively fewer in number, and held on successive days
    B. shorter, relatively greater in number, and spaced at intervals of several days
    C. of average length, relatively fewer in number, and held at intermittent intervals
    D. of random length and frequency, but spaced at fixed intervals

12.____

13. Employee training which is based on realistic simulation, sometimes known as *game play* or *role play*, is sometimes preferable to learning from actual experience on the job.
Which of the following is NOT a correct statement concerning the value of simulation to trainees?

13.____

A. Simulation allows for practice in decision-making without any need for subsequent discussion.
B. Simulation is intrinsically motivating because it offers a variety of challenges.
C. Compared to other, more traditional training techniques, simulation is dynamic.
D. The simulation environment is nonpunitive as compared to real life.

14. Programmed instruction as a method of training has all of the following advantages EXCEPT:
    A. Learning is accomplished in an optimum sequence of distinct steps.
    B. Trainees have wide latitude in deciding what is to be learned within each program.
    C. The trainee takes an active part in the learning process.
    D. The trainee receives immediate knowledge of the results of his response.

14.____

15. In a work-study program, trainees were required to submit weekly written performance reports in order to insure that work assignments fulfilled the program objectives.
    Such reports would also assist the administrator of the work-study program PRIMARILY to
    A. eliminate personal counseling for the trainees
    B. identify problems requiring prompt resolution
    C. reduce the amount of clerical work for all concerned
    D. estimate the rate at which budgeted funds are being expended

15.____

16. Which of the following would be MOST useful in order to avoid misunderstanding when preparing correspondence or reports?
    A. Use vocabulary which is at an elementary level
    B. Present each sentence as an individual paragraph
    C. Have someone other than the writer read the material for clarity
    D. Use general words which are open to interpretation

16.____

17. Which of the following supervisory methods would be MOST likely to train subordinates to give a prompt response to memoranda in an organizational setting where most transactions are informal?
    A. Issue a written directive setting forth a schedule of strict deadlines
    B. Let it be known, informally, that those who respond promptly will be rewarded
    C. Follow up each memorandum by a personal inquiry regarding the receiver's reaction to it
    D. Direct subordinates to furnish a precise explanation for ignoring memos

17.____

18. Conferences may fail for a number of reasons. Still, a conference that is an apparent failure may have some benefit.
    Which of the following would LEAST likely be such a benefit?
    It may
    A. increase for most participants their possessiveness about information they have

18.____

B. produce a climate of good will and trust among many of the participants
C. provide most participants with an opportunity to learn things about the others
D. serve as a unifying force to keep most of the individuals functioning as a group

19. Assume that you have been assigned to study and suggest improvements in an operating unit of a delegate agency whose staff has become overwhelmed with problems, has had inadequate resources, and has become accustomed to things getting worse. The staff is indifferent to cooperating with you because they see no hope of improvement.
Which of the following steps would be LEAST useful in carrying out your assignment?
    A. Encourage the entire staff to make suggestions to you for change
    B. Inform the staff that management is somewhat dissatisfied with their performance
    C. Let staff know that you are fully aware of their problems and stresses
    D. Look for those problem area where changes can be made quickly

19._____

20. Which of the following statements about employer-employee relations is NOT considered to be correct by leading managerial experts?
    A. An important factor in good employer-employee relations is treating workers respectfully.
    B. Employer-employee relations are profoundly influenced by the fundamentals of human nature.
    C. Good employer-employee relations must stem from top management and reach downward.
    D. Employee unions are usually a major obstacle to establishing good employer-employee relations.

20._____

21. In connection with labor relations, the term *management rights* GENERALLY refers to
    A. a managerial review system in a grievance system
    B. statutory prohibitions that bar monetary negotiations
    C. the impact of collective bargaining on government
    D. those subjects which management considers to be non-negotiable

21._____

22. Barriers may exist to the utilization of women in higher level positions. Some of these barriers are attitudinal in nature.
Which of the following is MOST clearly attitudinal in nature?
    A. Advancement opportunities which are vertical in nature and thus require seniority
    B. Experience which is inadequate or irrelevant to the needs of a dynamic and progressive organization
    C. Inadequate means of early identification of employees with talent and potential for advancement
    D. Lack of self-confidence on the part of some women concerning their ability to handle a higher position

22._____

23. Because a reader reacts to the meaning he associates with a word, we can neve be sure what emotional impact a word may carry or how it may affect our readers.
    The MOST logical implication of this statement for employees who correspond with members of the public is that
    A. a writer should try to select a neutral word that will not bias his writing by its hidden emotional meaning
    B. simple language should be used in writing letters denying requests so that readers are not upset by the denial
    C. every writer should adopt a writing style which he finds natural and easy
    D. whenever there is doubt as to how a word is defined, the dictionary should be consulted

24. A public information program should be based on clear information about the nature of actual public knowledge and opinion. One way of learning about the views of the public is through the use of questionnaires.
    Which of the following is of LEAST importance in designing a questionnaire?
    A. A respondent should be asked for his name and address.
    B. A respondent should be asked to choose from among several statements the one which expresses his views.
    C. Questions should ask for responses in a form suitable for processing.
    D. Questions should be stated in familiar language.

25. Assume that you have accepted an invitation to speak before an interested group about a problem. You have brought with you for distribution a number of booklets and other informational material.
    Of the following, which would be the BEST way to use this material?
    A. Distribute it before you begin talking so that the audience may read it at their leisure.
    B. Distribute it during your talk to increase the likelihood that it will be read.
    C. Hold it until the end of your talk, then announce that those who wish may take or examine the material.
    D. Before starting the talk, leave it on a table in the back of the room so that people may pick it up as they enter.

KEY (CORRECT ANSWERS)

1.	A	11.	C
2.	D	12.	B
3.	A	13.	A
4.	A	14.	B
5.	B	15.	B
6.	D	16.	C
7.	A	17.	C
8.	C	18.	A
9.	C	19.	B
10.	B	20.	D

21. D
22. D
23. A
24. A
25. C

TEST 2

DIRECTIONS: Each question or incomplete statement is followed by several suggested answers or completions. Select the one that BEST answers the question or completes the statement. *PRINT THE LETTER OF THE CORRECT ANSWER IN THE SPACE AT THE RIGHT.*

1. Of the following, the FIRST step in planning an operation is to 1.____
   A. obtain relevant information
   B. identify the goal to be achieved
   C. consider possible alternatives
   D. make necessary assignments

2. A supervisor who is extremely busy performing routine tasks is MOST likely making INCORRECT use of what basic principle of supervision? 2.____
   A. Homogeneous Assignment
   B. Span of Control
   C. Work Distribution
   D. Delegation of Authority

3. Controls help supervisors to obtain information from which they can determine whether their staffs are achieving planned goals.
   Which one of the following would be LEAST useful as a control device? 3.____
   A. Employee diaries
   B. Organization charts
   C. Periodic inspections
   D. Progress charts

4. A certain employee has difficulty in effectively performing a particular portion of his routine assignments, but his overall productivity is average.
   As the direct supervisor of his individual, your BEST course of action would be to 4.____
   A. attempt to develop the man's capacity to execute the problematic facets of his assignments
   B. diversify the employee's work assignments in order to build up his confidence
   C. reassign the man to less difficult tasks
   D. request in a private conversation that the employee improve his work output

5. A supervisor who uses persuasion as a means of supervising a unit would GENERALLY also use which of the following practices to supervise his unit? 5.____
   A. Supervise and control the staff with an authoritative attitude to indicate that he is a *take-charge* individual
   B. Make significant changes in the organizational operations so as to improve job efficiency
   C. Remove major communication barriers between himself, subordinates, and management
   D. Supervise everyday operations while being mindful of the problems of his subordinates

6. Whenever a supervisor in charge of a unit delegate a routine task to a capable subordinate, he tells him exactly how to do it. 6.____

This practice is GENERALLY
- A. *desirable*, chiefly because good supervisors should be aware of the traits of their subordinates and delegate responsibilities to them accordingly
- B. *undesirable*, chiefly because only non-routine tasks should be delegated
- C. *desirable*, chiefly because a supervisor should frequently test the willingness of his subordinates to perform ordinary tasks
- D. *undesirable*, chiefly because a capable subordinate should usually be allowed to exercise his own discretion in doing a routine job

7. The one of the following activities through which a supervisor BEST demonstrates leadership ability is by
   - A. arranging periodic staff meetings in order to keep his subordinates informed about professional developments in the field
   - B. frequently issuing definite orders and directives which will lessen the need for subordinates to make decisions in handling any tasks assigned to them
   - C. devoting the major part of his time to supervising subordinates so as to simulate continuous improvement
   - D. setting aside time for self-development and research so as to improve the skills, techniques, and procedures of his unit

8. The following three statements relate to the supervision of employees:
   I. The assignment of difficult tasks that offer a challenge is more conducive to good morale than the assignment of easy tasks.
   II. The same general principles of supervision that apply to men are equally applicable to women.
   III. The best retraining program should cover all phases of an employee's work in a general manner.
   Which of the following choices list ALL of the above statements that are generally correct?
   A. II, III   B. I   C. I, II   D. I, II, III

9. Which of the following examples BEST illustrates the application of the *exception principle* as a supervisory technique?
   - A. A complex job is divided among several employees who work simultaneously to complete the whole job in a shorter time.
   - B. An employee is required to complete any task delegated to him to such an extent that nothing is left for the superior who delegated the task except to approve it.
   - C. A superior delegates responsibility to a subordinate but retains authority to make the final decisions.
   - D. A superior delegates all work possible to his subordinates and retains that which requires his personal attention or performance

10. Assume that you are a supervisor. Your immediate superior frequently gives orders to your subordinates without your knowledge.
    Of the following, the MOST direct and effective way for you to handle this problem is to

A. tell our subordinates to take orders only from you
B. submit a report to higher authority in which you cite specific instances
C. discuss it with your immediate superior
D. find out to what extent your authority and prestige as a supervisor have been affected

11. In an agency which has as its primary purpose the protection of the public against fraudulent business practices, which of the following would GENERALLY be considered an *auxiliary* or *staff* rather than a *line* function?
    A. Interviewing victims of frauds and advising them about their legal remedies
    B. Daily activities directed toward prevention of fraudulent business practices
    C. Keeping records and statistics about business violations reported and corrected
    D. Follow-up inspections by investigators after corrective action has been taken

12. A supervisor can MOST effectively reduce the spread of false rumors through the *grapevine* by
    A. identifying and disciplining any subordinate responsible for initiating such rumors
    B. keeping his subordinates informed as much as possible about matters affecting them
    C. denying false rumors which might tend to lower staff morale and productivity
    D. making sure confidential matters are kept secure from access by unauthorized employees

13. A supervisor has tried to learn about the background, education, and family relationships of his subordinates through observation, personal contact, and inspection of their personnel records.
    These supervisor actions are GENERALLY
    A. *inadvisable*, chiefly because they may lead to charges of favoritism
    B. *advisable*, chiefly because they may make him more popular with his subordinates
    C. *inadvisable*, chiefly because his efforts may be regarded as an invasion of privacy
    D. *advisable*, chiefly because the information may enable him to develop better understanding of each of his subordinates

14. In an emergency situation, when action must be taken immediately, it is BEST for the supervisor to give orders in the form of
    A. direct commands which are brief and precise
    B. requests, so that his subordinates will not become alarmed
    C. suggestions which offer alternative courses of action
    D. implied directives, so that his subordinates may use their judgment in carrying them out

15. When demonstrating a new and complex procedure to a group of subordinates, it is ESSENTIAL that a supervisor
    A. go slowly and repeat the steps involved at least once
    B. show the employees common errors and the consequences of such errors
    C. go through the process at the usual speed so that the employees can see the rate at which they should work
    D. distribute summaries of the procedure during the demonstration and instruct his subordinates to refer to them afterwards

15.____

16. After a procedures manual has been written and distributed,
    A. continuous maintenance work is necessary to keep the manual current
    B. it is best to issue new manuals rather than make changes in the original manual
    C. no changes should be necessary
    D. only major changes should be considered

16.____

17. Of the following, the MOST important criterion of effective report writing is
    A. eloquence of writing style
    B. the use of technical language
    C. to be brief and to the point
    D. to cover all details

17.____

18. The use of electronic data processing
    A. has proven unsuccessful in most organizations
    B. has unquestionable advantages for all organizations
    C. is unnecessary in most organizations
    D. should be decided upon only after careful feasibility studies by individual organizations

18.____

19. The PRIMARY purpose of work measurement is to
    A. design and install a wage incentive program
    B. determine who should be promoted
    C. establish a yardstick to determine extent of progress
    D. set up a spirit of competition among employee

19.____

20. The action which is MOST effective in gaining acceptance of a study by the agency which is being studied is
    A. a directive from the agency head to install a study based on recommendations included in a report
    B. a lecture-type presentation following approval of the procedure
    C. a written procedure in narrative form covering the proposed system with visual presentations and discussions
    D. procedural charts showing the *before* situation, forms, steps, etc., to the employees affected

20.____

21. Which organization principle is MOST closely related to procedural analysis and improvement?
    A. Duplication, overlapping, and conflict should be eliminated.
    B. Managerial authority should be clearly defined.
    C. The objectives of the organization should be clearly defined.
    D. Top management should be freed of burdensome detail.

22. Which one of the following is the MAJOR objective of operational audits?
    A. Detecting fraud
    B. Determining organization problems
    C. Determining the number of personnel needed
    D. Recommending opportunities for improving operating and management practices

23. Of the following, the formalization of organization structure is BEST achieved by
    A. a narrative description of the plan of organization
    B. functional charts
    C. job descriptions together with organization charts
    D. multi-flow charts

24. Budget planning is MOST useful when it achieves
    A. cost control
    B. forecast of receipts
    C. performance review
    D. personnel reduction

25. GENERALLY, in applying the principle of delegation in dealing with subordinates, a supervisor
    A. allows his subordinates to set up work goals and to fix the limits within which they can work
    B. allows his subordinates to set up work goals and then gives detailed orders as to how they are to be achieved
    C. makes relatively few decisions by himself and frames his orders in broad, general terms
    D. provides externalized motivation for his subordinate

KEY (CORRECT ANSWERS)

1. B
2. D
3. B
4. A
5. D

6. D
7. C
8. C
9. D
10. C

11. C
12. B
13. D
14. A
15. A

16. A
17. C
18. D
19. C
20. C

21. A
22. D
23. C
24. A
25. C

EXAMINATION SECTION
TEST 1

DIRECTIONS: Each question or incomplete statement is followed by several suggested answers or completions. Select the one that BEST answers the question or completes the statement. *PRINT THE LETTER OF THE CORRECT ANSWER IN THE SPACE AT THE RIGHT.*

1. When a supervisor requests a subordinate to prepare a report, he should not only indicate the areas to be covered in the report but should also indicate to the subordinate

    A. for whom it is intended and its purpose
    B. the conclusions he expects to reach
    C. the decision that he will make based on the facts presented
    D. why that subordinate was chosen to prepare it

    1.____

2. The MOST accurate of the following principles of education and learning for a supervisor to keep in mind when planning a training program for the assistant supervisors under her supervision is that

    A. assistant supervisors, like all other individuals, vary in the rate at which they learn new material and in the degree to which they can retain what they do learn
    B. experienced assistant supervisors who have the same basic college education and agency experience will be able to learn new material at approximately the same rate of speed
    C. the speed with which assistant supervisors can learn new material after the age of forty is half as rapid as at ages twenty to thirty
    D. with regard to any specific task, it is easier and takes less time to break an experienced assistant supervisor of old, unsatisfactory work habits than it is to teach him new, acceptable ones

    2.____

3. Assume that you are a supervisor and that you are planning to train a group of experienced investigators in certain specific skills which they need in their daily work.
The one of the following methods which may *generally* be expected to be MOST valuable in ascertaining the effectiveness of the training program is to

    A. administer an objective examination to these investigators prior to conducting the training program and an equivalent form of the examination after the program and compare the results
    B. evaluate and compare the work records of these investigators with regard to these skills prior to and after completion of the training program
    C. hold a staff meeting with the investigators after the training program is completed and allow them to discuss frankly their opinions of the values they derived from the various parts of the training
    D. prepare an objective and detailed questionnaire covering the program, have the investigators answer without identifying themselves, and analyze the answers given

    3.____

4. A supervisor has received orders for a work assignment to be carried out by his unit. He has firmly decided on methods for carrying out this assignment which he believes will lead to its completion both properly and expeditiously. He has no intention whatsoever of changing his mind. After he has reached his decision, he calls a staff conference to discuss various alternative methods of carrying out the assignments without making clear that he has already decided upon the method to be used.
To hold a conference of this type would GENERALLY be a

   A. *good* idea, ecause his subordinates are likely to carry the assignment through better if they believe that they devised the methods used
   B. *good* idea, because the staff will have the opportunity and be properly motivated to gain knowledge and experience in methodology without endangering staff performance
   C. *poor* idea, because it would be a failure on the part of the supervisor to show the firm leadership which his unit has a right to expect
   D. *poor* idea, because the discovery by the staff that they had not actually participated in deciding upon methods to be used would have an adverse effect upon their morale

5. Supervisors are frequently faced with the necessity of training old employees in new tasks. An employee inexperienced in a task is much more likely to make a mistake than one who is experienced in it.
In delegating authority to an old employee to perform a new task, a supervisor should GENERALLY

   A. delegate the authority as soon as the subordinate gains minimum competence, allowing him to make mistakes which will not do major damage to the client or to the agency program
   B. delegate the authority as soon as the subordinate gains minimum competence but supervise him closely, enough so that he will not have the opportunity to make even minor mistakes
   C. make the delegation of authority dependent upon the importance which the client places upon the problems involved
   D. withhold the authority until the employee has become experienced in performing the task

6. A supervisor has been transferred from supervision of one group of units to another group of units. She spends the first three weeks in her new assignment in getting acquainted with her new subordinates, their problems, and their work. In this process, she notices that some of the records and forms which are submitted to her by two of the assistant supervisors are carelessly or improperly prepared.
The BEST of the following actions for the supervisor to take in this situation is to

   A. carefully check the work submitted by these assistant supervisors during an additional three weeks before taking any more positive action
   B. confer with these offending workers and show each one where her work needs improvement and how to go about achieving it
   C. institute an in-service training program specifically designed to solve such a problem and instruct the entire subordinate staff in proper work methods
   D. make a note of these errors for documentary use in preparing the annual service rating reports and advise the workers involved to prepare their work more carefully

7. A supervisor, who was promoted to this position a year ago, has supervised a certain assistant supervisor for this one year. The work of the assistant supervisor has been very poor because he has done a minimum of work, refused to take sufficient responsibility, been difficult to handle, and required very close supervision. Apparently due to the increasing insistence by his supervisor that he improve the caliber of his work, the assistant supervisor tenders his resignation, stating that the demands of the job are too much for him. The opinion of the previous supervisor, who had supervised this assistant supervisor for two years, agrees substantially with that of the new supervisor. Under such circumstances, the BEST of the following actions the supervisor can take in general is to

   A. recommend that the resignation be accepted and that he be rehired should he later apply when he feels able to do the job
   B. recommend that the resignation be accepted and that he not be rehired should he later so apply
   C. refuse to accept the resignation but try to persuade the assistant supervisor to accept psychiatric help
   D. refuse to accept the resignation, promising the assistant supervisor that he will be less closely supervised in the future since he is now so experienced

8. After completing a conference with a supervisor concerning the ramifications of a complex problem, an employee informs the supervisor that she feels that her assistant supervisor is too strict in her handling of all the workers under her supervision, especially in comparison with the other assistant supervisors.
   The one of the following actions which is *generally* BEST for the supervisor to take is to

   A. advise the worker in a friendly fashion to apply for a transfer to a unit which has a more lenient supervisor
   B. caution the employee that complaining about a fellow employee behind her back is frowned upon by higher authority as it is a sign of disloyalty
   C. inform the employee that she, the supervisor, will investigate the complaint to determine whether or not it has any validity
   D. tell the worker that the closer and stricter a supervisor is, the better and more completely trained will be her subordinate staff

9. Rumors have arisen to the effect that one of the investigators under your supervision has been attending classes at a local university during afternoon hours when he is supposed to be making field visits.
   The BEST of the following ways for you to approach this problem is to

   A. disregard the rumors since, like most rumors, they probably have no actual foundation in fact
   B. have a discreet investigation made in order to determine the actual facts prior to taking any other action
   C. inform the investigator that you know what he has been doing and that such behavior is overt dereliction of duty and is punishable by dismissal
   D. review the investigator's work record, spot check his performance, and take no further action unless the quality of his work is below average for the unit

10. A supervisor must consider many factors in evaluating a worker whom he has supervised for a considerable time. In evaluating the capacity of such a worker to use independent judgment, the one of the following to which the supervisor should *generally* give MOST consideration is the worker's

A. capacity to establish good relationships with people (clients, colleagues)
B. educational background
C. emotional stability
D. the quality and judgment shown by the worker in previous work situations known to the supervisor

11. A supervisor is conducting a special meeting with the assistant supervisors under her supervision to read and discuss some major complex changes in the rules and procedures. She notices that one of the assistant supervisors who is normally attentive at meetings seems to be paying no attention to what is being said. The supervisor stops reading the rules and asks the assistant supervisor a couple of questions about the changed procedure, to which she gets satisfactory answers.
The BEST action of the following for the supervisor to take at the meeting is to

    A. advise the assistant supervisor gently but firmly that these changes are complex and that her undivided attention is required in order to fully comprehend them
    B. avoid further embarrassment to the assistant supervisor by asking the group as a whole to pay more attention to what is being read
    C. discontinue the questioning and resume reading the procedure
    D. politely request the assistant supervisor to stop giving those present the impression that she is uninterested in what goes on about her

12. A supervisor becomes aware that one of her very competent experienced workers never takes notes during an interview with a client except to note an occasional name, address, or date. When asked about this practice by the supervisor, the worker states that she has a good memory for important details and has always been able to satisfactorily record an interview after the client has left.
It would *generally* be BEST for the supervisor to handle this situation by

    A. discussing with her that more extensive note-taking may sometimes be desirable with a client who believes note-taking to be evidence that his problem will receive serious consideration
    B. agreeing with this practice since note-taking interferes with the establishment of a proper worker-client relationship
    C. explaining that, since interviewing is an art form rather than an exact science, a good worker must devise her own personal rules for interviewing and not be bound by general principles
    D. warning the worker that memory is too uncertain a thing to be relied upon and, therefore, notes should be taken during an interview of all matters

13. When an experienced subordinate who has the authority and information necessary to make a decision on a certain difficult matter brings the matter to his supervisor without having made the decision, it would *generally* be BEST for the supervisor to

    A. agree to make the decision for the subordinate after the subordinate has explained why he finds it difficult to make the decision and after he has made a recommendation
    B. make the decision for the subordinate, explaining to him the reasons for arriving at the decision
    C. refuse to make the decision, but discuss the various alternatives with the subordinate in order to clarify the issues involved
    D. refuse to make the decision, explaining to the subordinate that he is deemed to be fully qualified and competent to make the decision

14. The one of the following instances when it is MOST important for an upper-level supervisor to follow the chain of command is when he is

    A. communicating decisions
    B. communicating information
    C. receiving suggestions
    D. seeking information

15. Experts in the field of personnel relations feel that it is generally a bad practice for subordinate employees to become aware of pending or contemplated changes in policy or organizational set-up via the *grapevine* CHIEFLY because

    A. evidence that one or more responsible officials have proved untrustworthy will undermine confidence in the agency
    B. the information disseminated by this method is seldom entirely accurate and generally spreads needless unrest among the subordinate staff
    C. the subordinate staff may conclude that the administration feels the staff cannot be trusted with the true information
    D. the subordinate staff may conclude that the administration lacks the courage to make an unpopular announcement through official channels

16. In order to maintain a proper relationship with a worker who is assigned to staff rather than line functions, a line supervisor should

    A. accept all recommendations of the staff worker
    B. include the staff worker in the conferences called by the supervisor for his subordinates
    C. keep the staff worker informed of developments in the area of his staff assignment
    D. require that the staff worker's recommendations be communicated to the supervisor through the supervisor's own superior

17. Of the following, the GREATEST disadvantage of placing a worker in a staff position under the direct supervision of the supervisor whom he advises is the possibility that the

    A. staff worker will tend to be insubordinate because of a feeling of superiority over the supervisor
    B. staff worker will tend to give advice of the type which the supervisor wants to hear or finds acceptable
    C. supervisor will tend to be mistrustful of the advice of a worker of subordinate rank
    D. supervisor will tend to derive little benefit from the advice because to supervise properly he should know at least as much as his subordinate

18. One factor which might be given consideration in deciding upon the optimum span of control of a supervisor over his immediate subordinates is the position of the supervisor in the hierarchy of the organization.
    It is GENERALLY considered proper that the number of subordinates immediately supervised by a higher, upper echelon supervisor

    A. is unrelated to and tends to form no pattern with the number supervised by lower-level supervisors
    B. should be about the same as the number supervised by a lower-level supervisor
    C. should be larger than the number supervised by a lower-level supervisor
    D. should be smaller than the number supervised by a lower-level supervisor

19. An important administrative problem is how precisely to define the limits on authority that is delegated to subordinate supervisors.
    Such definition of limits of authority should be

    A. as precise as possible and practicable in all areas
    B. as precise as possible and practicable in areas of function, but should allow considerable flexibility in the area of personnel management
    C. as precise as possible and practicable in the area of personnel management, but should allow considerable flexibility in the areas of function
    D. in general terms so as to allow considerable flexibility both in the areas of function and in the areas of personnel management

20. The LEAST important of the following reasons why a particular activity should be assigned to a unit which performs activities dissimilar to it is that

    A. close coordination is needed between the particular activity and other activities performed by the unit
    B. it will enhance the reputation and prestige of the unit supervisor
    C. the unit makes frequent use of the results of this particular activity
    D. the unit supervisor has a sound knowledge and understanding of the particular activity

21. In a conference on difficult cases between a recently appointed supervisor and an experienced, above-average employee, the MOST valuable of the following services that the supervisor can offer the employee is a

    A. detached point of view
    B. knowledge of human needs
    C. knowledge of the agency's basic rules and regulations
    D. willingness to make decisions

22. A supervisor is put in charge of a special unit. She is exceptionally well qualified for this assignment by her training and experience. One of her very close personal friends has been working for some time in this unit. Both the supervisor and worker are certain that the rest of the employees in the unit, many of whom have been in the bureau for a long time, know of this close relationship.
    Under these circumstances, the MOST advisable action for the supervisor to take is to

    A. ask that either she be allowed to return to her old assignment or, if that cannot be arranged, that her friend be transferred to another unit in the center
    B. avoid any overt sign of favoritism by acting impartiall and with greater reserve when dealing with this employee than with the rest of the staff
    C. discontinue any socializing with this employee either inside or outside the office so as to eliminate any gossip or dissatisfaction
    D. talk the situation over with the employee and arrive at a mutually acceptable plan of proper office decorum

23. A supervisor who wishes to attain established objectives should concentrate on

    A. determining whether management is operating at maximum effectiveness
    B. making suggestions for improving the organization
    C. planning work assignments
    D. securing salary increases for needy employees

24. A usually competent employee complains that he does not understand the procedures to be followed in performing a certain task although the supervisor has explained them twice and has demonstrated them.
Of the following, the BEST course of action for the supervisor to take is to

   A. ask the employee whether he has any problems which are bothering him
   B. assign someone else to the job
   C. explain the procedures again and demonstrate at the same time
   D. have the employee perform the job while he watches and gives additional instructions

25. GENERALLY, in order to be completely qualified as a supervisor, a person

   A. should be able to perform exceptionally well at least one of the jobs he supervises and have some knowledge of the others
   B. must have an intimate working knowledge of all facets of the jobs which he supervises
   C. should know the basic principles and procedures of the jobs he supervises
   D. need know little or nothing of the jobs which he supervises as long as he knows the principles of supervision

KEY (CORRECT ANSWERS)

1. A
2. A
3. B
4. D
5. A

6. B
7. B
8. C
9. B
10. D

11. C
12. A
13. C
14. A
15. B

16. C
17. B
18. D
19. A
20. B

21. A
22. A
23. C
24. D
25. C

TEST 2

DIRECTIONS: Each question or incomplete statement is followed by several suggested answers or completions. Select the one that BEST answers the question or completes the statement. *PRINT THE LETTER OF THE CORRECT ANSWER IN THE SPACE AT THE RIGHT.*

1. Your superior has asked you to notify employees of an important change in one of the operating procedures described in the manual. Every employee presently has a copy of this manual.
   Which of the following is *normally* the MOST practical way to get the employees to understand such a change?

    A. Notify each employee individually of the change and answer any questions he might have
    B. Send a written notice to key personnel, directing them to inform the people under them
    C. Call a general meeting, distribute a corrected page for the manual, and discuss the change
    D. Send a memo to employees describing the change in general terms and asking them to make the necessary corrections in their copies of the manual

2. A supervisor was directed by the head of his division to report figures for overtime wages. The supervisor asked a clerk under his supervision to give him the figures, and he passed the clerk's figures along to his superior without questioning them. It was then discovered that the clerk had carelessly supplied the wrong information. Who can PROPERLY be held responsible for the mistake, the supervisor or the payroll clerk?

    A. Only the supervisor because he should have known that the clerk would be careless
    B. Only the clerk because it should be unnecessary for supervisors to check the work of their subordinates except for work which is unusually complex or important
    C. Neither of them because it is perfectly understandable that such mistakes will occur from time to time
    D. Both of them because the person to whom a task is delegated is responsible to the supervisor who delegated the task, and the supervisor is responsible to his superior

3. As a supervisor, it is necessary for you to show a new employee how to enter information on standard forms that he will have to prepare. These forms have a number of blanks to be filled in, but the job is fairly simple once a person becomes familiar with it.
   The BEST way to show the new employee how to do the job is to

    A. explain how to do it and have him fill out a few forms, helping him with any difficulties
    B. give him a completed form to use as a model and tell him to do all the others exactly the same way
    C. put him on his own immediately and assume that he will learn for himself through trial and error
    D. give him several dozen completed forms to read and ask him to check back with you in a few hours when he feels ready to start work

4. Suppose that a usually competent employee whom you supervise has suddenly begun having difficulty completing his assignments. You ask the employee to speak to you privately about this situation, and he agrees that he would appreciate this opportunity because of a problem he is having.
Of the following, which one would be the BEST technique for you to use in speaking with him?

   A. Criticize the employee's performance as soon as he mentions his difficulty in completing his assignments
   B. Listen patiently to what the employee has to say before making any comments on your own
   C. Refuse to discuss any personal factors which the employee mentions when he tries to explain his recent work difficulty
   D. Allow the employee to argue with you but plan your attack and defense carefully

5. A certain supervisor does not compliment members of his staff when they come up with good ideas. He feels that coming up with good ideas is part of the job and does not merit special attention.
This supervisor's practice is

   A. *poor,* because recognition for good ideas is a good motivator
   B. *poor,* because the staff will suspect that the supervisor has no good ideas of his own
   C. *good,* because it is reasonable to assume that employees will tell their supervisor of ways to improve office practice
   D. *good,* because the other members of the staff are not made to seem inferior by comparison

6. An employee under your supervision complains about a decision you have made in assigning work in the office. You consider the matter to be unimportant, but it seems to be very important to him. He is excited and very angry. Of the following, the MOST appropriate action for you to take FIRST is to

   A. listen to the details of his complaint
   B. refer him to your superior
   C. tell him to *cool off* before discussing the matter
   D. tell him to settle it with the other employees

7. An experienced employee complains to his unit supervisor that the latter's continual, very close supervision of his work is unnecessary and annoying. The unit supervisor has been recently appointed.
Of the following, it would *generally* be BEST for the unit supervisor to

   A. agree to discontinue all supervision if the employee will agree, if he has any problems, to consult the supervisor
   B. assure the employee that close supervision is necessary but should not be taken personally
   C. consider with the employee what aspects of the supervision could be reduced
   D. explain that he is supervising closely only until he learns what the job is all about

8. A supervisor had a clerk assigned to help him review records. One day the supervisor asked the clerk to continue checking the records, and the clerk said, *No, I'm not doing any more of that today.*
   In this instance, the supervisor should IMMEDIATELY

   A. ask the clerk why he will not check the records
   B. ask another clerk to do the job
   C. tell the clerk he must do it or be transferred
   D. contact his own supervisor

8.___

9. Assume that you have been assigned to supervise other employees. You find that one of your subordinates makes many mistakes whenever he prepares a particular report. Of the following, the MOST desirable course of action for you to follow FIRST in such a situation is to

   A. retrain the subordinate in the preparation of the report
   B. transfer the subordinate to another unit
   C. tell the subordinate to improve or resign
   D. give the employee different duties

9.___

10. Some employees of a department have sent an anonymous letter containing many complaints to the department head. Of the following, what is this MOST likely to show about the department?

    A. It is probably a good place to work.
    B. Communications are probably poor.
    C. The complaints are probably unjustified.
    D. These employees are probably untrustworthy.

10.___

11. Of the following, the BEST reason for rotating employee work assignments is that such rotation

    A. challenges the ingenuity of supervisors in making assignments
    B. gives each employee a chance at both desirable and undesirable assignments
    C. creates specialists among all employees
    D. increases the competitive spirit among employees

11.___

12. Although an employee under your supervision frequently protests when receiving a monotonous assignment, he nevertheless performs the assigned task efficiently. His protests, however, disturb the other employees and interfere with their work.
    Of the following actions you may take in handling this employee, the MOST desirable one is for you to

    A. point out to him the effect of his conduct on the staff's work and request his cooperation in accepting such assignments
    B. arrange to issue such assignments to him when the other members of the staff are not present
    C. inform him that you will request his transfer to another unit unless he puts a halt to his unjustifiable protests
    D. ask other members of the staff to tell him that he is disturbing them by his protests

12.___

13. A supervisor has had several problems with a clerk who assists him. He calls the clerk in for a discussion of the matters.
    Which of the following should comprise the MAJOR part of the discussion?

    A. All the things the clerk has done wrong
    B. The most recent things the clerk has done wrong
    C. The things the clerk has done well in addition to the things he has done wrong
    D. The clerk's previous experience and personal problems

14. Assume that certain work processed in your office is then sent to another office for further processing. One of the employees in your office tells you that the supervisor in the other office has been complaining about your office's method of handling the work.
    Of the following, the MOST appropriate action for you to take is to

    A. get all the details from the employee and then speak to the other supervisor
    B. ignore the situation and continue to do the best you can
    C. remind the supervisor that it is not his function to evaluate your work
    D. refrain from reporting the matter to your superior

15. It is the practice in your department to make objective evaluations of the performance of different units. This requires looking at the results achieved by a particular unit during a specified period of time; for instance, the number of applications processed, the number of inquiries answered, the number of inspections made, and so forth.
    Of the following, the BEST method of evaluating the performance of each unit is to compare its results with the

    A. results achieved by all units of the same size that are performing other kinds of work
    B. goals that the unit was reasonably expected to meet during the specified period
    C. performance of the same unit during a similar period of time four or five years earlier
    D. amount of money spent to achieve these results

16. It is possible that you may be asked to submit a brief written evaluation of the work of several employees under your supervision.
    Such an evaluation should *normally* give LEAST emphasis to an employee's

    A. attendance record, including tardiness and absence
    B. ability to grasp new assignments and carry them out effectively
    C. educational background and previous employment experience
    D. ability to get along with co-workers

17. Of the following leadership characteristics, the one that is *generally* considered PRIMARY for a supervisor is the ability to

    A. achieve good working relations with fellow supervisors
    B. get subordinates to air their personal problems
    C. take action to get the job done
    D. plan his work efficiently

18. A recently appointed supervisor is placed in charge of a district which includes several senior employees. He finds that while these subordinates are able to learn new tasks and methods, some of them tend to take longer to learn procedural changes than newer, younger workers.
Of the following, the MAIN reason for this is that senior workers

   A. are embarrassed by younger workers' intelligence
   B. have to *unlearn* what was taught them in the past
   C. form learning blocks when they are supervised by a younger person
   D. are more interested in doing the work than in academic discussions

19. Which of the following is *generally* considered to be the MOST desirable way for a supervisor to begin a discussion of an employee's performance with the employee?

   A. Accentuate the positive by giving credit where credit is due
   B. Encourage the employee to suggest ways in which he can improve
   C. Point out specific instances of poor performance
   D. Suggest training programs that the employee may be interested in

20. For a supervisor to use consultative supervision with his subordinates effectively, it is ESSENTIAL that he

   A. accept the fact that his formal authority will be weakened by the procedure
   B. admit that he does not know more than all his men together and that his ideas are not always best
   C. utilize a committee system so that the procedure is orderly
   D. make sure that all subordinates are consulted so that no one feels left out

21. During a conversation with his supervisor, a subordinate begins to discuss what appears to the supervisor to be a deep-seated personality problem that has been bothering the subordinate.
For the supervisor to suggest to the subordinate the possibility of professional help would NORMALLY be

   A. *undesirable;* the necessity of requiring professional help would automatically disqualify the subordinate from being promoted in the future
   B. *desirable;* generally a supervisor can be of limited assistance in personally solving deep-seated personality problems
   C. *undesirable;* since the supervisor was approached by the employee, it is his responsibility as a supervisor to help the employee solve his problem
   D. *desirable;* in accordance with the Civil Service Commission regulations, a supervisor is not allowed to get involved in subordinates' personal problems

22. When a new method of performing a job operation is to be instituted, the one of the following approaches which will MOST generally gain acceptance of the change by subordinates is to

   A. hold a friendly, informal meeting after the change has been implemented to explain the advantages of the new method
   B. consult the subordinates involved in the change as early as possible in the planning stage
   C. work closely with just one of the subordinates who will be affected by the change so that others need not be taken off the job

D. implement the change, instruct employees fully in the new method, and then follow up on results

23. Of the following, the supervisory practice which is LEAST likely to produce a favorable work environment is that the supervisor   23._____

    A. takes an active interest in subordinates
    B. does not tolerate mistakes, regardless of who has made the mistake
    C. gives praise when justified
    D. disciplines individuals in accordance with their violation of the rules

24. When a supervisor finds it necessary to let a subordinate know that he is dissatisfied with the subordinate's level of performance, which of the following tactics would *usually* prove MOST effective in improving the subordinate's performance?   24._____

    A. The supervisor should be angry when criticizing in order to prevent the mistakes from recurring.
    B. Once criticism has been made, the supervisor should be sure to continuously impress the seriousness of the mistakes upon the subordinate.
    C. When making his criticism, the supervisor should guard against referring to any work that was well done since this would reduce the effect of his criticism.
    D. The supervisor should focus his criticism on the mistakes being made and should avoid downgrading the subordinate personally.

25. Of the following, the BEST descriptive statement of an effective supervisor is *generally* that he   25._____

    A. works alongside his subordinates on the same type of work
    B. catches all errors when they are made
    C. gives many specific work orders and few general work orders
    D. devotes much of his time to long-range activities, such as planning and improving human relations

KEY (CORRECT ANSWERS)

1. C
2. D
3. A
4. B
5. A

6. A
7. C
8. A
9. A
10. B

11. B
12. A
13. C
14. A
15. B

16. C
17. C
18. B
19. A
20. D

21. B
22. B
23. B
24. D
25. D

PREPARING WRITTEN MATERIAL
EXAMINATION SECTION
TEST 1

DIRECTIONS: Each of the sentences in this test may be classified under one of the following four categories:
  A. Faulty because of incorrect grammar or word usage
  B. Faulty because of incorrect punctuation
  C. Faulty because of incorrect capitalization or incorrect spelling
  D. Correct

Examine each sentence carefully to determine under which of the above four options it is best classified. Then, in the space to the right, print the capital letter preceding the option which is the BEST of the four suggested above. (Note that each faulty sentence contains but one type of error. Consider a sentence to be correct if it contains none of the types of errors mentioned, even though there may be other correct ways of expressing the same thought.)

1. He sent the notice to the clerk who you hired yesterday.   1.____

2. It must be admitted, however that you were not informed of this change.   2.____

3. Only the employee who have served in this grade for at least two years are eligible for promotion.   3.____

4. The work was divided equally between she and Mary.   4.____

5. He thought that you were not available at that time.   5.____

6. When the messenger returns; please give him this package.   6.____

7. The new secretary prepared, typed, addressed, and delivered, the notices.   7.____

8. Walking into the room, his desk can be seen at the rear.   8.____

9. Although John has worked here longer than She, he produces a smaller amount of work.   9.____

10. She said she could of typed this report yesterday.   10.____

11. Neither one of these procedures are adequate for the efficient performance of this task.   11.____

12. The typewriter is the tool of the typist; the cash register, the tool of the cashier.   12.____

13. "The assignment must be completed as soon as possible" said the supervisor.   13.____

14. As you know, office handbooks are issued to all new Employees.   14.____

15. Writing a speech is sometimes easier than to deliver it before an audience.   15.____

16. Mr. Brown our accountant, will audit the accounts next week.   16.____

17. Give the assignment to whomever is able to do it most efficiently.   17.____

18. The supervisor expected either your or I to file these reports.   18.____

KEY (CORRECT ANSWERS)

1. A 11. A
2. B 12. C
3. D 13. B
4. A 14. C
5. D 15. A

6. B 16. B
7. B 17. A
8. A 18. A
9. C
10. A

TEST 2

DIRECTIONS: Each of the sentences in this test may be classified under one of the following four categories:
  A. Faulty because of incorrect grammar or word usage
  B. Faulty because of incorrect punctuation
  C. Faulty because of incorrect capitalization or incorrect spelling
  D. Correct

Examine each sentence carefully to determine under which of the above four options it is best classified. Then, in the space to the right, print the capital letter preceding the option which is the BEST of the four suggested above. (Note that each faulty sentence contains but one type of error. Consider a sentence to be correct if it contains none of the types of errors mentioned, even though there may be other correct ways of expressing the same thought.)

1. The fire apparently started in the storeroom, which is usually locked. 1.____
2. On approaching the victim, two bruises were noticed by this officer. 2.____
3. The officer, who was there examined the report with great care. 3.____
4. Each employee in the office had a seperate desk. 4.____
5. All employees including members of the clerical staff, were invited to the lecture. 5.____
6. The suggested Procedure is similar to the one now in use. 6.____
7. No one was more pleased with the new procedure than the chauffeur. 7.____
8. He tried to persaude her to change the procedure. 8.____
9. The total of the expenses charged to petty cash were high. 9.____
10. An understanding between him and I was finally reached. 10.____

KEY (CORRECT ANSWERS)

1. D   6. C
2. A   7. D
3. B   8. C
4. C   9. A
5. B   10. A

TEST 3

DIRECTIONS: Each of the sentences in this test may be classified under one of the following four categories:
- A. Faulty because of incorrect grammar or word usage
- B. Faulty because of incorrect punctuation
- C. Faulty because of incorrect capitalization or incorrect spelling
- D. Correct

Examine each sentence carefully to determine under which of the above four options it is best classified. Then, in the space to the right, print the capital letter preceding the option which is the BEST of the four suggested above. (Note that each faulty sentence contains but one type of error. Consider a sentence to be correct if it contains none of the types of errors mentioned, even though there may be other correct ways of expressing the same thought.)

1. They told both he and I that the prisoner had escaped. 1.____

2. Any superior officer, who, disregards the just complaint of his subordinates, is remiss in the performance of his duty. 2.____

3. Only those members of the national organization who resided in the Middle West attended the conference in Chicago. 3.____

4. We told him to give the national organization assignment to whoever was available. 4.____

5. Please do not disappoint and embarass us by not appearing in court. 5.____

6. Although the office's speech proved to be entertaining, the topic was not relevent to the main theme of the conference. 6.____

7. In February all new officers attended a training course in which they were learned in their principal duties and the fundamental operating procedure of the department. 7.____

8. I personally seen inmate Jones threaten inmates Smith and Green with bodily harm if they refused to participate in the plot. 8.____

9. To the layman, who on a chance visit to the prison observes everything functioning smoothly, the maintenance of prison discipline may seem to be a relatively easily realizable objective. 9.____

10. The prisoners in cell block fourty were forbidden to sit on the cell cots during the recreation hour. 10.____

KEY (CORRECT ANSWERS)

1. A   6. C
2. B   7. A
3. C   8. A
4. D   9. D
5. C   10. C

TEST 4

DIRECTIONS: Each of the sentences in this test may be classified under one of the following four categories:
- A. Faulty because of incorrect grammar or word usage
- B. Faulty because of incorrect punctuation
- C. Faulty because of incorrect capitalization or incorrect spelling
- D. Correct

Examine each sentence carefully to determine under which of the above four options it is best classified. Then, in the space to the right, print the capital letter preceding the option which is the BEST of the four suggested above. (Note that each faulty sentence contains but one type of error. Consider a sentence to be correct if it contains none of the types of errors mentioned, even though there may be other correct ways of expressing the same thought.)

1. I cannot encourage you any. 1._____
2. You always look well in those sort of clothes. 2._____
3. Shall we go to the park? 3._____
4. The man whome he introduced was Mr. Carey. 4._____
5. She saw the letter laying here this morning. 5._____
6. It should rain before the Afternoon is over. 6._____
7. They have already went home. 7._____
8. That Jackson will be elected is evident. 8._____
9. He does not hardly approve of us. 9._____
10. It was he, who won the prize. 10._____

KEY (CORRECT ANSWERS)

1.	A	6.	C
2.	A	7.	A
3.	D	8.	D
4.	C	9.	A
5.	A	10.	B

TEST 5

DIRECTIONS: Each of the sentences in this test may be classified under one of the following four categories:
  A. Faulty because of incorrect grammar or word usage
  B. Faulty because of incorrect punctuation
  C. Faulty because of incorrect capitalization or incorrect spelling
  D. Correct

Examine each sentence carefully to determine under which of the above four options it is best classified. Then, in the space to the right, print the capital letter preceding the option which is the BEST of the four suggested above. (Note that each faulty sentence contains but one type of error. Consider a sentence to be correct if it contains none of the types of errors mentioned, even though there may be other correct ways of expressing the same thought.)

1. Shall we go to the park. 1.____
2. They are, alike, in this particular way. 2.____
3. They gave the poor man sume food when he knocked on the door. 3.____
4. I regret the loss caused by the error. 4.____
5. The students' will have a new teacher. 5.____
6. They sweared to bring out all the facts. 6.____
7. He decided to open a branch store on 33rd street. 7.____
8. His speed is equal and more than that of a racehorse. 8.____
9. He felt very warm on that Summer day. 9.____
10. He was assisted by his friend, who lives in the next house. 10.____

KEY (CORRECT ANSWERS)

1. B   6. A
2. B   7. C
3. C   8. A
4. D   9. C
5. B   10. D

TEST 6

DIRECTIONS: Each of the sentences in this test may be classified under one of the following four categories:
- A. Faulty because of incorrect grammar or word usage
- B. Faulty because of incorrect punctuation
- C. Faulty because of incorrect capitalization or incorrect spelling
- D. Correct

Examine each sentence carefully to determine under which of the above four options it is best classified. Then, in the space to the right, print the capital letter preceding the option which is the BEST of the four suggested above. (Note that each faulty sentence contains but one type of error. Consider a sentence to be correct if it contains none of the types of errors mentioned, even though there may be other correct ways of expressing the same thought.)

1. The climate of New York is colder than California.   1._____
2. I shall wait for you on the corner.   2._____
3. Did we see the boy who, we think, is the leader.   3._____
4. Being a modest person, John seldom talks about his invention.   4._____
5. The gang is called the smith street bos.   5._____
6. He seen the man break into the store.   6._____
7. We expected to lay still there for quite a while.   7._____
8. He is considered to be the Leader of his organization.   8._____
9. Although I recieved an invitation, I won't go.   9._____
10. The letter must be here some place.   10._____

KEY (CORRECT ANSWERS)

1.	A	6.	A
2.	D	7.	A
3.	B	8.	C
4.	D	9.	C
5.	C	10.	A

TEST 7

DIRECTIONS: Each of the sentences in this test may be classified under one of the following four categories:
   A. Faulty because of incorrect grammar or word usage
   B. Faulty because of incorrect punctuation
   C. Faulty because of incorrect capitalization or incorrect spelling
   D. Correct

Examine each sentence carefully to determine under which of the above four options it is best classified. Then, in the space to the right, print the capital letter preceding the option which is the BEST of the four suggested above. (Note that each faulty sentence contains but one type of error. Consider a sentence to be correct if it contains none of the types of errors mentioned, even though there may be other correct ways of expressing the same thought.)

1. I though it to be he. 1._____
2. We expect to remain here for a long time. 2._____
3. The committee was agreed. 3._____
4. Two-thirds of the building are finished. 4._____
5. The water was froze. 5._____
6. Everyone of the salesmen must supply their own car. 6._____
7. Who is the author of Gone With the Wind? 7._____
8. He marched on and declaring that he would never surrender. 8._____
9. Who shall I say called? 9._____
10. Everyone has left but they. 10._____

KEY (CORRECT ANSWERS)

1.	A	6.	A
2.	D	7.	B
3.	D	8.	A
4.	A	9.	D
5.	A	10.	D

TEST 8

DIRECTIONS: Each of the sentences in this test may be classified under one of the following four categories:
- A. Faulty because of incorrect grammar or word usage
- B. Faulty because of incorrect punctuation
- C. Faulty because of incorrect capitalization or incorrect spelling
- D. Correct

Examine each sentence carefully to determine under which of the above four options it is best classified. Then, in the space to the right, print the capital letter preceding the option which is the BEST of the four suggested above. (Note that each faulty sentence contains but one type of error. Consider a sentence to be correct if it contains none of the types of errors mentioned, even though there may be other correct ways of expressing the same thought.)

1. Who did we give the order to?   1.____
2. Send your order in immediately.   2.____
3. I believe I paid the Bill.   3.____
4. I have not met but one person.   4.____
5. Why aren't Tom, and Fred, going to the dance?   5.____
6. What reason is there for him not going?   6.____
7. The seige of Malta was a tremendous event.   7.____
8. I was there yesterday I assure you   8.____
9. Your ukulele is better than mine.   9.____
10. No one was there only Mary.   10.____

KEY (CORRECT ANSWERS)

1.	A	6.	A
2.	D	7.	C
3.	C	8.	B
4.	A	9.	C
5.	B	10.	A

TEST 9

DIRECTIONS: In each of the following groups of sentences, one of the four sentences is faulty in grammar, punctuation, or capitalization. Select the INCORRECT sentence in each case.

1. A. If you had stood at home and done your homework, you would not have failed in arithmetic.
    B. Her affected manner annoyed every member of the audience.
    C. How will the new law affect our income taxes?
    D. The plants were not affected by the long, cold winter, but they succumbed to the drought of summer.

    1.____

2. A. He is one of the most able men who have been in the Senate.
    B. It is he who is to blame for the lamentable mistake.
    C. Haven't you a helpful suggestion to make at this time?
    D. The money was robbed from the blind man's cup.

    2.____

3. A. The amount of children in this school is steadily increasing.
    B. After taking an apple from the table, she went out to play.
    C. He borrowed a dollar from me.
    D. I had hoped my brother would arrive before me.

    3.____

4. A. Whom do you think I hear from every week?
    B. Who do you think is the right man for the job?
    C. Who do you think I found in the room?
    D. He is the man whom we considered a good candidate for the presidency.

    4.____

5. A. Quietly the puppy laid down before the fireplace.
    B. You have made your bed; now lie in it.
    C. I was badly sunburned because I had lain too long in the sun.
    D. I laid the doll on the bed and left the room.

    5.____

KEY (CORRECT ANSWERS)

1. A
2. D
3. A
4. C
5. A

PREPARING WRITTEN MATERIAL

PARAGRAPH REARRANGEMENT
COMMENTARY

The sentences that follow are in scrambled order. You are to rearrange them in proper order and indicate the letter choice containing the correct answer at the space at the right.

Each group of sentences in this section is actually a paragraph presented in scrambled order. Each sentence in the group has a place in that paragraph; no sentence is to be left out. You are to read each group of sentences and decide upon the best order in which to put the sentences so as to form a well-organized paragraph.

The questions in this section measure the ability to solve a problem when all the facts relevant to its solution are not given.

More specifically, certain positions of responsibility and authority require the employee to discover connection between events sometimes, apparently, unrelated. In order to do this, the employee will find it necessary to correctly infer that unspecified events have probably occurred or are likely to occur. This ability becomes especially important when action must be taken on incomplete information.

Accordingly, these questions require competitors to choose among several suggested alternatives, each of which presents a different sequential arrangement of the events. Competitors must choose the MOST logical of the suggested sequences.

In order to do so, they may be required to draw on general knowledge to infer missing concepts or events that are essential to sequencing the given events. Competitors should be careful to infer only what is essential to the sequence. The plausibility of the wrong alternatives will always require the inclusion of unlikely events or of additional chains of events which are NOT essential to sequencing the given events.

It's very important to remember that you are looking for the best of the four possible choices, and that the best choice of all may not even be one of the answers you're given to choose from.

There is no one right way to solve these problems. Many people have found it helpful to first write out the order of the sentences, as they would have arranged them, on their scrap paper before looking at the possible answers. If their optimum answer is there, this can save them some time. If it isn't, this method can still give insight into solving the problem. Others find it most helpful to just go through each of the possible choices, contrasting each as they go along. You should use whatever method feels comfortable and works for you.

While most of these types of questions are not that difficult, we've added a higher percentage of the difficult type, just to give you more practice. Usually there are only one or two questions on this section that contain such subtle distinctions that you're unable to answer confidently. And you then may find yourself stuck deciding between two possible choices, neither of which you're sure about.

EXAMINATION SECTION
TEST 1

DIRECTIONS: The sentences that follow are in scrambled order. You are to rearrange them in proper order and indicate the letter choice containing the correct answer. *PRINT THE LETTER OF THE CORRECT ANSWER IN THE SPACE AT THE RIGHT.*

1. Below are four statements labeled W, X, Y and Z.
   W. He was a strict and fanatic drillmaster.
   X. The word is always used in a derogatory sense and generally shows resentment and anger on the part of the user.
   Y. It is from the name of this Frenchman that we derive our English word, martinet.
   Z. Jean Martinet was the Inspector-General of Infantry during the reign of King Louis XIV.
   The PROPER order in which these sentences should be placed in a paragraph is:
   A. X, Z, W, Y   B. X, Z, Y, W   C. Z, W, Y, X   D. Z, Y, W, X

   1.____

2. In the following paragraph, the sentences, which are numbered, have been jumbled.
   I. Since then it has undergone changes.
   II. It was incorporated in 1955 under the laws of the State of New York.
   III. Its primary purposes, a cleaner city, has, however, remained the same.
   IV. The Citizens Committee works in cooperation with the Mayor's Inter-departmental Committee for a Clean City.
   The order in which these sentences should be arranged to form a well-organized paragraph is:
   A. II, IV, I, III   B. III, IV, I, II   C. IV, II, I, III   D. IV, III, II, I

   2.____

   3.____

Questions 3-5.

DIRECTIONS: The sentences listed below are part of a meaningful paragraph but they are not given in their proper order. You are to decide what would be the BEST order in which to put the sentences so as to form a well-organized paragraph. Each sentence has a place in the paragraph; there are no extra sentences. You are then to answer Questions 3 through 5 inclusive on the basis of your rearrangements of these scrambled sentences into a properly organized paragraph.

In 1887 some insurance companies organized an Inspection Department to advise their clients on all phases of fire prevention and protection. Probably this has been due to the smaller annual fire losses in Great Britain than in the United States. It tests various fire prevention devices and appliances and determines manufacturing hazards and their safeguards. Fire research began earlier in the United States and is more advanced than in Great Britain. Later they established a laboratory specializing in electrical, mechanical, hydraulic, and chemical fields.

171

2 (#1)

3. When the five sentences are arranged in proper order, the paragraph starts with the sentence which begins 3.____
    A. "In 1887..."   B. "Probably this..."   C. "It tests..."
    D. "Fire research..."   E. "Later they..."

4. In the last sentence listed above, "they" refers to 4.____
    A. the insurance companies   B. the United States and Great Britain
    C. the Inspection Department   D. clients
    E. technicians

5. When the above paragraph is properly arranged, it ends with the words 5.____
    A. "...and protection."   B. "...the United States."
    C. "...their safeguards."   D. "...in Great Britain."
    E. "...chemical fields."

KEY (CORRECT ANSWERS)

1. C
2. C
3. D
4. A
5. C

TEST 2

DIRECTIONS: In each of the questions numbered I through V, several sentences are given. For each question, choose as your answer the group of number that represents the MOST logical order of these sentences if they were arranged in paragraph form. *PRINT THE LETTER OF THE CORRECT ANSWER IN THE SPACE AT THE RIGHT.*

1.
   I. It is established when one shows that the landlord has prevented the tenant's enjoyment of his interest in the property leased.
   II. Constructive eviction is the result of a breach of the covenant of quiet enjoyment implied in all leases.
   III. In some parts of the United States, it is not complete until the tenant vacates within a reasonable time.
   IV. Generally, the acts must be of such serious and permanent character as to deny the tenant the enjoyment of his possessing rights.
   V. In this event, upon abandonment of the premises, the tenant's liability for that ceases.
   The CORRECT answer is:
   A. II, I, IV, III, V
   B. V, II, III, I, IV
   C. IV, III, I, II, V
   D. I, III, V, IV, II

   1.____

2.
   I. The powerlessness before private and public authorities that is the typical experience of the slum tenant is reminiscent of the situation of blue-collar workers all through the nineteenth century.
   II. Similarly, in recent years, this chapter of history has been reopened by anti-poverty groups which have attempted to organize slum tenants to enable them to bargain collectively with their landlords about the conditions of their tenancies.
   III. It is familiar history that many of the worker remedied their condition by joining together and presenting their demands collectively.
   IV. Like the workers, tenants are forced by the conditions of modern life into substantial dependence on these who possess great political aid and economic power.
   V. What's more, the very fact of dependence coupled with an absence of education and self-confidence makes them hesitant and unable to stand up for what they need from those in power.
   The CORRECT answer is:
   A. V, IV, I, II, III
   B. II, III, I, V, IV
   C. III, I, V, IV, II
   D. I, IV, V, III, II

   2.____

3.
   I. A railroad, for example, when not acting as a common carrier may contract away responsibility for its own negligence.
   II. As to a landlord, however, no decision has been found relating to the legal effect of a clause shifting the statutory duty of repair to the tenant.
   III. The courts have not passed on the validity of clauses relieving the landlord of this duty and liability.
   IV. They have, however, upheld the validity of exculpatory clauses in other types of contracts.

   3.____

173

V. Housing regulations impose a duty upon the landlord to maintain leased premises in safe condition.
VI. As another example, a bailee may limit his liability except for gross negligence, willful acts, or fraud.
The CORRECT answer is:
A. II, I, VI, IV, III, V
B. I, III, IV, V, VI, II
C. III, V, I, IV, II, VI
D. V, III, IV, I, VI, II

4. I. Since there are only samples in the building, retail or consumer sales are generally eschewed by mart occupants, and in some instances, rigid controls are maintained to limit entrance to the mart only to those persons engaged in retailing.
II. Since World War I, in many larger cities, there has developed a new type of property, called the mart building.
III. It can, therefore, be used by wholesalers and jobbers for the display of sample merchandise.
IV. This type of building is most frequently a multi-storied, finished interior property which is a cross between a retail arcade and a loft building.
V. This limitation enables the mart occupants to ship the orders from another location after the retailer or dealer makes his selection from the samples.
The CORRECT answer is:
A. II, IV, III, I, V
B. IV, III, V, I, II
C. I, III, II, IV, V
D. I, IV, II, III, V

5. I. In general, staff-line friction reduces the distinctive contribution of staff personnel.
II. The conflicts, however, introduce an uncontrolled element into the managerial system.
III. On the other hand, the natural resistance of the line to staff innovations probably usefully restrains over-eager efforts to apply untested procedures on a large scale.
IV. Under such conditions, it is difficult to know when valuable ideas are being sacrificed.
V. The relatively weak position of staff, requiring accommodation to the line, tends to restrict their ability to engage in free, experimental innovation.
The CORRECT answer is:
A. IV, II, III, I, V
B. I, V, III, II, IV
C. V, III, I, II, IV
D. II, I, IV, V, III

KEY (CORRECT ANSWERS)

1. A
2. D
3. D
4. A
5. B

TEST 3

DIRECTIONS: Questions 1 through 4 consist of six sentences which can be arranged in a logical sequence. For each question, select the choice which places the numbered sentences in the MOST logical sequent. *PRINT THE LETTER OF THE CORRECT ANSWER IN THE SPACE AT THE RIGHT.*

1. I. The burden of proof as to each issue is determined before trial and remains upon the same party throughout the trial.
    II. The jury is at liberty to believe one witness' testimony as against a number of contradictory witnesses.
    III. In a civil case, the party bearing the burden of proof is required to prove his contention by a fair preponderance of the evidence.
    IV. However, it must be noted that a fair preponderance of evidence does not necessarily mean a greater number of witnesses.
    V. The burden of proof is the burden which rests upon one of the parties to an action to persuade the trier of the facts, generally the jury, that a proposition he asserts is true.
    VI. If the evidence is equally balanced, or if it leaves the jury in such doubt as to be unable to decide the controversy either way, judgment must be given against the party upon whom the burden of proof rests.
    The CORRECT answer is:
    A. III, II, V, IV, I, VI
    B. I, II, VI, V, III, IV
    C. III, IV, V, I, II, VI
    D. V, I, III, VI, IV, II

    1.____

2. I. If a parent is without assets and is unemployed, he cannot be convicted of the crime of non-support of a child.
    II. The term "sufficient ability" has been held to mean sufficient financial ability.
    III. It does not matter if his unemployment is by choice or unavoidable circumstances.
    IV. If he fails to take any steps at all, he may be liable to prosecution for endangering the welfare of a child.
    V. Under the penal law, a parent is responsible for the support of his minor child only if the parent is "of sufficient ability."
    VI. An indigent parent may meet his obligation by borrowing money or by seeking aid under the provisions of the Social Welfare Law.
    The CORRECT answer is:
    A. VI, I, V, III, II, IV
    B. I, III, V, II, IV, VI
    C. V, II, I, III, VI, IV
    D. I, VI, IV, V, II, III

    2.____

3. I. Consider, for example, the case of a rabble rouser who urges a group of twenty people to go out and break the windows of a nearby factory.
    II. Therefore, the law fills the indicated gap with the crime of inciting to riot.
    III. A person is considered guilty of inciting to riot when he urges ten or more persons to engage in tumultuous and violent conduct of a kind likely to create public alarm.
    IV. However, if he has not obtained the cooperation of at least four people, he cannot be charged with unlawful assembly.

    3.____

175

V. The charge of inciting to riot was added to the law to cover types of conduct which cannot be classified as either the crime of "riot" or the crime of "unlawful assembly."
VI. If he acquires the acquiescence of at least four of them, he is guilty of unlawful assembly even if the project does not materialize.

The CORRECT answer is:
A. III, V, I, VI, IV, II
B. V, I, IV, VI, II, III
C. III, IV, I, V, II, VI
D. V, I, IV, VI, III, II

4. I. If, however, the rebuttal evidence presents an issue of credibility, it is for the jury to determine whether the presumption has, in fact, been destroyed.
    II. Once sufficient evidence to the contrary is introduced, the presumption disappears from the trial.
    III. The effect of a presumption is to place the burden upon the adversary to come forward with evidence to rebut the presumption.
    IV. When a presumption is overcome and ceases to exist in the case, the fact or facts which gave rise to the presumption still remain.
    V. Whether a presumption has been overcome is ordinarily a question for the court.
    VI. Such information may furnish a basis for a logical inference.

The CORRECT answer is:
A. IV, VI, II, V, I, III
B. III, II, V, I, IV, VI
C. V, III, VI, IV, II, I
D. V, IV, I, II, VI, III

KEY (CORRECT ANSWERS)

1. D
2. C
3. A
4. B

PHILOSOPHY, PRINCIPLES, PRACTICES, AND TECHNICS OF SUPERVISION, ADMINISTRATION, MANAGEMENT, AND ORGANIZATION

TABLE OF CONTENTS

	Page
MEANING OF SUPERVISION	1
THE OLD AND THE NEW SUPERVISION	1
THE EIGHT (8) BASIC PRINCIPLES OF THE NEW SUPERVISION	1
I. Principle of Responsibility	1
II. Principle of Authority	2
III. Principle of Self-Growth	2
IV. Principle of Individual Worth	2
V. Principle of Creative Leadership	2
VI. Principle of Success and Failure	2
VII. Principle of Science	3
VIII. Principle of Cooperation	3
WHAT IS ADMINISTRATION?	3
I. Practices Commonly Classed as "Supervisory"	3
II. Practices Commonly Classed as "Administrative"	3
III. Practices Commonly Classed as Both "Supervisory" and "Administrative"	4
RESPONSIBILITIES OF THE SUPERVISOR	4
COMPETENCIES OF THE SUPERVISOR	4
THE PROFESSIONAL SUPERVISOR-EMPLOYEE RELATIONSHIP	4
MINI-TEXT IN SUPERVISION, ADMINISTRATION, MANAGEMENT, AND ORGANIZATION	5
I. Brief Highlights	5
A. Levels of Management	6
B. What the Supervisor Must Learn	6
C. A Definition of Supervision	6
D. Elements of the Team Concept	6
E. Principles of Organization	6
F. The Four Important Parts of Every Job	7
G. Principles of Delegation	7
H. Principles of Effective Communications	7
I. Principles of Work Improvement	7
J. Areas of Job Improvement	7
K. Seven Key Points in Making Improvements	8

	L.	Corrective Techniques for Job Improvement	8
	M.	A Planning Checklist	8
	N.	Five Characteristics of Good Directions	9
	O.	Types of Directions	9
	P.	Controls	9
	Q.	Orienting the New Employee	9
	R.	Checklist for Orienting New Employees	9
	S.	Principles of Learning	10
	T.	Causes of Poor Performance	10
	U.	Four Major Steps in On-the-Job Instructions	10
	V.	Employees Want Five Things	10
	W.	Some Don'ts in Regard to Praise	11
	X.	How to Gain Your Workers' Confidence	11
	Y.	Sources of Employee Problems	11
	Z.	The Supervisor's Key to Discipline	11
	AA.	Five Important Processes of Management	12
	BB.	When the Supervisor Fails to Plan	12
	CC.	Fourteen General Principles of Management	12
	DD.	Change	12
II.	Brief Topical Summaries		13
	A.	Who/What is the Supervisor?	13
	B.	The Sociology of Work	13
	C.	Principles and Practices of Supervision	14
	D.	Dynamic Leadership	14
	E.	Processes for Solving Problems	15
	F.	Training for Results	15
	G.	Health, Safety, and Accident Prevention	16
	H.	Equal Employment Opportunity	16
	I.	Improving Communications	16
	J.	Self-Development	17
	K.	Teaching and Training	17
		1. The Teaching Process	17
		a. Preparation	17
		b. Presentation	18
		c. Summary	18
		d. Application	18
		e. Evaluation	18
		2. Teaching Methods	18
		a. Lecture	18
		b. Discussion	18
		c. Demonstration	19
		d. Performance	19
		e. Which Method to Use	19

PHILOSOPHY, PRINCIPLES, PRACTICES, AND TECHNICS OF SUPERVISION, ADMINISTRATION, MANAGEMENT, AND ORGANIZATION

MEANING OF SUPERVISION

The extension of the democratic philosophy has been accompanied by an extension in the scope of supervision. Modern leaders and supervisors no longer think of supervision in the narrow sense of being confined chiefly to visiting employees, supplying materials, or rating the staff. They regard supervision as being intimately related to all the concerned agencies of society, they speak of the supervisor's function in terms of "growth," rather than the "improvement" of employees.

This modern concept of supervision may be defined as follows: Supervision is leadership and the development of leadership within groups which are cooperatively engaged in inspection, research, training, guidance, and evaluation.

THE OLD AND THE NEW SUPERVISION

TRADITIONAL
1. Inspection
2. Focused on the employee
3. Visitation
4. Random and haphazard
5. Imposed and authoritarian
6. One person usually

MODERN
1. Study and analysis
2. Focused on aims, materials, methods, supervisors, employees, environment
3. Demonstrations, intervisitation, workshops, directed reading, bulletins, etc.
4. Definitely organized and planned (scientific)
5. Cooperative and democratic
6. Many persons involved (creative)

THE EIGHT (8) BASIC PRINCIPLES OF THE NEW SUPERVISION

I. Principle of Responsibility
   Authority to act and responsibility for acting must be joined.
   A. If you give responsibility, give authority.
   B. Define employee duties clearly.
   C. Protect employees from criticism by others.
   D. Recognize the rights as well as obligations of employees.
   E. Achieve the aims of a democratic society insofar as it is possible within the area of your work.
   F. Establish a situation favorable to training and learning.
   G. Accept ultimate responsibility for everything done in your section, unit, office, division, department.
   H. Good administration and good supervision are inseparable.

II. Principle of Authority
The success of the supervisor is measured by the extent to which the power of authority is not used.
- A. Exercise simplicity and informality in supervision
- B. Use the simplest machinery of supervision
- C. If it is good for the organization as a whole, it is probably justified.
- D. Seldom be arbitrary or authoritative.
- E. Do not base your work on the power of position or of personality.
- F. Permit and encourage the free expression of opinions.

III. Principle of Self-Growth
The success of the supervisor is measured by the extent to which, and the speed with which, he is no longer needed.
- A. Base criticism on principles, not on specifics.
- B. Point out higher activities to employees.
- C. Train for self-thinking by employees to meet new situations.
- D. Stimulate initiative, self-reliance, and individual responsibility
- E. Concentrate on stimulating the growth of employees rather than on removing defects.

IV. Principle of Individual Worth
Respect for the individual is a paramount consideration in supervision.
- A. Be human and sympathetic in dealing with employees.
- B. Don't nag about things to be done.
- C. Recognize the individual differences among employees and seek opportunities to permit best expression of each personality.

V. Principle of Creative Leadership
The best supervision is that which is not apparent to the employee.
- A. Stimulate, don't drive employees to creative action.
- B. Emphasize doing good things.
- C. Encourage employees to do what they do best.
- D. Do not be too greatly concerned with details of subject or method.
- E. Do not be concerned exclusively with immediate problems and activities.
- F. Reveal higher activities and make them both desired and maximally possible.
- G. Determine procedures in the light of each situation but see that these are derived from a sound basic philosophy.
- H. Aid, inspire, and lead so as to liberate the creative spirit latent in all good employees.

VI. Principle of Success and Failure
There are no unsuccessful employees, only unsuccessful supervisors who have failed to give proper leadership.
- A. Adapt suggestions to the capacities, attitudes, and prejudices of employees.
- B. Be gradual, be progressive, be persistent.
- C. Help the employee find the general principle; have the employee apply his own problem to the general principle.
- D. Give adequate appreciation for good work and honest effort.
- E. Anticipate employee difficulties and help to prevent them.
- F. Encourage employees to do the desirable things they will do anyway.
- G. Judge your supervision by the results it secures.

VII. Principle of Science
Successful supervision is scientific, objective, and experimental. It is based on facts, not on prejudices.
   A. Be cumulative in results.
   B. Never divorce your suggestions from the goals of training.
   C. Don't be impatient of results.
   D. Keep all matters on a professional, not a personal, level.
   E. Do not be concerned exclusively with immediate problems and activities.
   F. Use objective means of determining achievement and rating where possible.

VIII. Principle of Cooperation
Supervision is a cooperative enterprise between supervisor and employee.
   A. Begin with conditions as they are.
   B. Ask opinions of all involved when formulating policies.
   C. Organization is as good as its weakest link.
   D. Let employees help to determine policies and department programs.
   E. Be approachable and accessible—physically and mentally.
   F. Develop pleasant social relationships.

WHAT IS ADMINISTRATION

Administration is concerned with providing the environment, the material facilities, and the operational procedures that will promote the maximum growth and development of supervisors and employees. (Organization is an aspect and a concomitant of administration.)

There is no sharp line of demarcation between supervision and administration; these functions are intimately interrelated and, often, overlapping. They are complementary activities.

I. Practices Commonly Classed as "Supervisory"
   A. Conducting employees' conferences
   B. Visiting sections, units, offices, divisions, departments
   C. Arranging for demonstrations
   D. Examining plans
   E. Suggesting professional reading
   F. Interpreting bulletins
   G. Recommending in-service training courses
   H. Encouraging experimentation
   I. Appraising employee morale
   J. Providing for intervisitation

II. Practices Commonly Classified as "Administrative"
   A. Management of the office
   B. Arrangement of schedules for extra duties
   C. Assignment of rooms or areas
   D. Distribution of supplies
   E. Keeping records and reports
   F. Care of audio-visual materials
   G. Keeping inventory records
   H. Checking record cards and books

      I.   Programming special activities
      J.   Checking on the attendance and punctuality of employees

III.   Practices Commonly Classified as Both "Supervisory" and "Administrative"
      A.   Program construction
      B.   Testing or evaluating outcomes
      C.   Personnel accounting
      D.   Ordering instructional materials

RESPONSIBILITIES OF THE SUPERVISOR

A person employed in a supervisory capacity must constantly be able to improve his own efficiency and ability. He represent the employer to the employees and only continuous self-examination can make him a capable supervisor.

Leadership and training are the supervisor's responsibility. An efficient working unit is one in which the employees work with the supervisor. It is his job to bring out the best in his employees. He must always be relaxed, courteous, and calm in his association with his employees. Their feelings are important, and a harsh attitude does not develop the most efficient employees.

COMPETENCES OF THE SUPERVISOR

I.   Complete knowledge of the duties and responsibilities of his position.
II.   To be able to organize a job, plan ahead, and carry through.
III.   To have self-confidence and initiative.
IV.   To be able to handle the unexpected situation and make quick decisions.
V.   To be able to properly train subordinates in the positions they are best suited for.
VI.   To be able to keep good human relations among his subordinates.
VII.   To be able to keep good human relations between his subordinates and himself and to earn their respect and trust.

THE PROFESSIONAL SUPERVISOR-EMPLOYEE RELATIONSHIP

There are two kinds of efficiency: one kind is only apparent and is produced in organizations through the exercise of mere discipline; this is but a simulation of the second, or true, efficiency which springs from spontaneous cooperation. If you are a manager, no matter how great or small your responsibility, it is your job, in the final analysis, to create and develop this involuntary cooperation among the people whom you supervise. For, no matter how powerful a combination of money, machines, and materials a company may have, this is a dead and sterile thing without a team of willing, thinking, and articulate people to guide it.

The following 21 points are presented as indicative of the exemplary basic relationship that should exist between supervisor and employee:

1. Each person wants to be liked and respected by his fellow employee and wants to be treated with consideration and respect by his superior.
2. The most competent employee will make an error. However, in a unit where good relations exist between the supervisor and his employees, tenseness and fear do not exist. Thus, errors are not hidden or covered up, and the efficiency of a unit is not impaired.

3. Subordinates resent rules, regulations, or orders that are unreasonable or unexplained.
4. Subordinates are quick to resent unfairness, harshness, injustices, and favoritism.
5. An employee will accept responsibility if he knows that he will be complimented for a job well done, and not too harshly chastised for failure; that his supervisor will check the cause of the failure, and, if it was the supervisor's fault, he will assume the blame therefore. If it was the employee's fault, his supervisor will explain the correct method or means of handling the responsibility.
6. An employee wants to receive credit for a suggestion he has made, that is used. If a suggestion cannot be used, the employee is entitled to an explanation. The supervisor should not say "no" and close the subject.
7. Fear and worry slow up a worker's ability. Poor working environment can impair his physical and mental health. A good supervisor avoids forceful methods, threats, and arguments to get a job done.
8. A forceful supervisor is able to train his employees individually and as a team, and is able to motivate them in the proper channels.
9. A mature supervisor is able to properly evaluate his subordinates and to keep them happy and satisfied.
10. A sensitive supervisor will never patronize his subordinates.
11. A worthy supervisor will respect his employees' confidences.
12. Definite and clear-cut responsibilities should be assigned to each executive.
13. Responsibility should always be coupled with corresponding authority.
14. No change should be made in the scope or responsibilities of a position without a definite understanding to that effect on the part of all persons concerned.
15. No executive or employee, occupying a single position in the organization, should be subject to definite orders from more than one source.
16. Orders should never be given to subordinates over the head of a responsible executive. Rather than do this, the officer in question should be supplanted.
17. Criticisms of subordinates should, whoever possible, be made privately, and in no case should a subordinate be criticized in the presence of executives or employees of equal or lower rank.
18. No dispute or difference between executives or employees as to authority or responsibilities should be considered too trivial for prompt and careful adjudication.
19. Promotions, wage changes, and disciplinary action should always be approved by the executive immediately superior to the one directly responsible.
20. No executive or employee should ever be required, or expected, to be at the same time an assistant to, and critic of, another.
21. Any executive whose work is subject to regular inspection should, wherever practicable, be given the assistance and facilities necessary to enable him to maintain an independent check of the quality of his work.

MINI-TEXT IN SUPERVISION, ADMINISTRATION, MANAGEMENT, AND ORGANIZATION

I. Brief Highlights

Listed concisely and sequentially are major headings and important data in the field for quick recall and review.

A. Levels of Management
Any organization of some size has several levels of management. In terms of a ladder, the levels are:

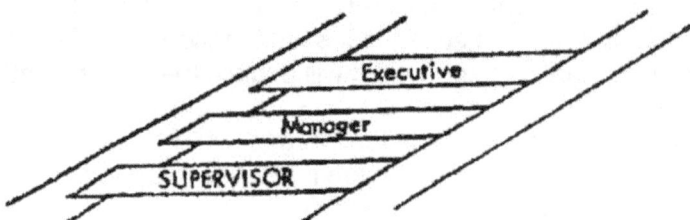

The first level is very important because it is the beginning point of management leadership.

B. What the Supervisor Must Learn
A supervisor must learn to:
1. Deal with people and their differences
2. Get the job done through people
3. Recognize the problems when they exist
4. Overcome obstacles to good performance
5. Evaluate the performance of people
6. Check his own performance in terms of accomplishment

C. A Definition of Supervisor
The term supervisor means any individual having authority, in the interests of the employer, to hire, transfer, suspend, lay-off, recall, promote, discharge, assign, reward, or discipline other employees or responsibility to direct them, or to adjust their grievances, or effectively to recommend such action, if, in connection with the foregoing, exercise of such authority is not of a merely routine or clerical nature but requires the use of independent judgment.

D. Elements of the Team Concept
What is involved in teamwork? The component parts are:
1. Members
2. A leader
3. Goals
4. Plans
5. Cooperation
6. Spirit

E. Principles of Organization
1. A team member must know what his job is.
2. Be sure that the nature and scope of a job are understood.
3. Authority and responsibility should be carefully spelled out.
4. A supervisor should be permitted to make the maximum number of decisions affecting his employees.
5. Employees should report to only one supervisor.
6. A supervisor should direct only as many employees as he can handle effectively.
7. An organization plan should be flexible.

8. Inspection and performance of work should be separate.
9. Organizational problems should receive immediate attention.
10. Assign work in line with ability and experience.

F. The Four Important Parts of Every Job
1. Inherent in every job is the *accountability* for results.
2. A second set of factors in every job is *responsibilities*.
3. Along with duties and responsibilities one must have the *authority* to act within certain limits without obtaining permission to proceed.
4. No job exists in a vacuum. The supervisor is surrounded by key *relationships*.

G. Principles of Delegation
Where work is delegated for the first time, the supervisor should think in terms of these questions:
1. Who is best qualified to do this?
2. Can an employee improve his abilities by doing this?
3. How long should an employee spend on this?
4. Are there any special problems for which he will need guidance?
5. How broad a delegation can I make?

H. Principles of Effective Communications
1. Determine the media.
2. To whom directed?
3. Identification and source authority.
4. Is communication understood?

I. Principles of Work Improvement
1. Most people usually do only the work which is assigned to them.
2. Workers are likely to fit assigned work into the time available to perform it.
3. A good workload usually stimulates output.
4. People usually do their best work when they know that results will be reviewed or inspected.
5. Employees usually feel that someone else is responsible for conditions of work, workplace layout, job methods, type of tools/equipment, and other such factors.
6. Employees are usually defensive about their job security.
7. Employees have natural resistance to change.
8. Employees can support or destroy a supervisor.
9. A supervisor usually earns the respect of his people through his personal example of diligence and efficiency.

J. Areas of Job Improvement
The areas of job improvement are quite numerous, but the most common ones which a supervisor can identify and utilize are:
1. Departmental layout
2. Flow of work
3. Workplace layout
4. Utilization of manpower
5. Work methods
6. Materials handling

7. Utilization
8. Motion economy

K. Seven Key Points in Making Improvements
1. Select the job to be improved
2. Study how it is being done now
3. Question the present method
4. Determine actions to be taken
5. Chart proposed method
6. Get approval and apply
7. Solicit worker participation

L. Corrective Techniques of Job Improvement
Specific Problems
1. Size of workload
2. Inability to meet schedules
3. Strain and fatigue
4. Improper use of men and skills
5. Waste, poor quality, unsafe conditions
6. Bottleneck conditions that hinder output
7. Poor utilization of equipment and machine
8. Efficiency and productivity of labor

General Improvement
1. Departmental layout
2. Flow of work
3. Work plan layout
4. Utilization of manpower
5. Work methods
6. Materials handling
7. Utilization of equipment
8. Motion economy

Corrective Techniques
1. Study with scale model
2. Flow chart study
3. Motion analysis
4. Comparison of units produced to standard allowance
5. Methods analysis
6. Flow chart and equipment study
7. Down time vs. running time
8. Motion analysis

M. A Planning Checklist
1. Objectives
2. Controls
3. Delegations
4. Communications
5. Resources
6. Manpower

7. Equipment
8. Supplies and materials
9. Utilization of time
10. Safety
11. Money
12. Work
13. Timing of improvements

N. Five Characteristics of Good Directions
In order to get results, directions must be:
1. Possible of accomplishment
2. Agreeable with worker interests
3. Related to mission
4. Planned and complete
5. Unmistakably clear

O. Types of Directions
1. Demands or direct orders
2. Requests
3. Suggestion or implication
4. volunteering

P. Controls
A typical listing of the overall areas in which the supervisor should establish controls might be:
1. Manpower
2. Materials
3. Quality of work
4. Quantity of work
5. Time
6. Space
7. Money
8. Methods

Q. Orienting the New Employee
1. Prepare for him
2. Welcome the new employee
3. Orientation for the job
4. Follow-up

R. Checklist for Orienting New Employees   Yes   No
1. Do you appreciate the feelings of new employees
   when they first report for work?   ___   ___
2. Are you aware of the fact that the new employee must
   make a big adjustment to his job?   ___   ___
3. Have you given him good reasons for liking the job and
   the organization?   ___   ___
4. Have you prepared for his first day on the job?   ___   ___
5. Did you welcome him cordially and make him feel needed?   ___   ___

		Yes	No

6. Did you establish rapport with him so that he feels free to talk and discuss matters with you? ___ ___
7. Did you explain his job to him and his relationship to you? ___ ___
8. Does he know that his work will be evaluated periodically on a basis that is fair and objective? ___ ___
9. Did you introduce him to his fellow workers in such a way that they are likely to accept him? ___ ___
10. Does he know what employee benefits he will receive? ___ ___
11. Does he understand the importance of being on the job and what to do if he must leave his duty station? ___ ___
12. Has he been impressed with the importance of accident prevention and safe practice? ___ ___
13. Does he generally know his way around the department? ___ ___
14. Is he under the guidance of a sponsor who will teach the right way of doing things? ___ ___
15. Do you plan to follow-up so that he will continue to adjust successfully to his job? ___ ___

S. Principles of Learning
   1. Motivation
   2. Demonstration or explanation
   3. Practice

T. Causes of Poor Performance
   1. Improper training for job
   2. Wrong tools
   3. Inadequate directions
   4. Lack of supervisory follow-up
   5. Poor communications
   6. Lack of standards of performance
   7. Wrong work habits
   8. Low morale
   9. Other

U. Four Major Steps in On-The-Job Instruction
   1. Prepare the worker
   2. Present the operation
   3. Tryout performance
   4. Follow-up

V. Employees Want Five Things
   1. Security
   2. Opportunity
   3. Recognition
   4. Inclusion
   5. Expression

W. Some Don'ts in Regard to Praise
1. Don't praise a person for something he hasn't done.
2. Don't praise a person unless you can be sincere.
3. Don't be sparing in praise just because your superior withholds it from you.
4. Don't let too much time elapse between good performance and recognition of it

X. How to Gain Your Workers' Confidence
Methods of developing confidence include such things as:
1. Knowing the interests, habits, hobbies of employees
2. Admitting your own inadequacies
3. Sharing and telling of confidence in others
4. Supporting people when they are in trouble
5. Delegating matters that can be well handled
6. Being frank and straightforward about problems and working conditions
7. Encouraging others to bring their problems to you
8. Taking action on problems which impede worker progress

Y. Sources of Employee Problems
On-the-job causes might be such things as:
1. A feeling that favoritism is exercised in assignments
2. Assignment of overtime
3. An undue amount of supervision
4. Changing methods or systems
5. Stealing of ideas or trade secrets
6. Lack of interest in job
7. Threat of reduction in force
8. Ignorance or lack of communications
9. Poor equipment
10. Lack of knowing how supervisor feels toward employee
11. Shift assignments

Off-the-job problems might have to do with:
1. Health
2. Finances
3. Housing
4. Family

Z. The Supervisor's Key to Discipline
There are several key points about discipline which the supervisor should keep in mind:
1. Job discipline is one of the disciplines of life and is directed by the supervisor.
2. It is more important to correct an employee fault than to fix blame for it.
3. Employee performance is affected by problems both on the job and off.
4. Sudden or abrupt changes in behavior can be indications of important employee problems.
5. Problems should be dealt with as soon as possible after they are identified.
6. The attitude of the supervisor may have more to do with solving problems than the techniques of problem solving.
7. Correction of employee behavior should be resorted to only after the supervisor is sure that training or counseling will not be helpful.

12

  8. Be sure to document your disciplinary actions.
  9. Make sure that you are disciplining on the basis of facts rather than personal feelings.
  10. Take each disciplinary step in order, being careful not to make snap judgments, or decisions based on impatience.

AA. Five Important Processes of Management
  1. Planning
  2. Organizing
  3. Scheduling
  4. Controlling
  5. Motivating

BB. When the Supervisor Fails to Plan
  1. Supervisor creates impression of not knowing his job
  2. May lead to excessive overtime
  3. Job runs itself—supervisor lacks control
  4. Deadlines and appointments missed
  5. Parts of the work go undone
  6. Work interrupted by emergencies
  7. Sets a bad example
  8. Uneven workload creates peaks and valleys
  9. Too much time on minor details at expense of more important tasks

CC. Fourteen General Principles of Management
  1. Division of work
  2. Authority and responsibility
  3. Discipline
  4. Unity of command
  5. Unity of direction
  6. Subordination of individual interest to general interest
  7. Remuneration of personnel
  8. Centralization
  9. Scalar chain
  10. Order
  11. Equity
  12. Stability of tenure of personnel
  13. Initiative
  14. Esprit de corps

DD. Change

Bringing about change is perhaps attempted more often, and yet less well understood, than anything else the supervisor does. How do people generally react to change? (People tend to resist change that is imposed upon them by other individuals or circumstances.

Change is characteristic of every situation. It is a part of every real endeavor where the efforts of people are concerned.

1. Why do people resist change?
   People may resist change because of:
   a. Fear of the unknown
   b. Implied criticism
   c. Unpleasant experiences in the past
   d. Fear of loss of status
   e. Threat to the ego
   f. Fear of loss of economic stability

2. How can we best overcome the resistance to change?
   In initiating change, take these steps:
   a. Get ready to sell
   b. Identify sources of help
   c. Anticipate objections
   d. Sell benefits
   e. Listen in depth
   f. Follow up

II. Brief Topical Summaries

   A. Who/What is the Supervisor?
      1. The supervisor is often called the "highest level employee and the lowest level manager."
      2. A supervisor is a member of both management and the work group. He acts as a bridge between the two.
      3. Most problems in supervision are in the area of human relations, or people problems.
      4. Employees expect: Respect, opportunity to learn and to advance, and a sense of belonging, and so forth.
      5. Supervisors are responsible for directing people and organizing work. Planning is of paramount importance.
      6. A position description is a set of duties and responsibilities inherent to a given position.
      7. It is important to keep the position description up-to-date and to provide each employee with his own copy.

   B. The Sociology of Work
      1. People are alike in many ways; however, each individual is unique.
      2. The supervisor is challenged in getting to know employee differences. Acquiring skills in evaluating individuals is an asset.
      3. Maintaining meaningful working relationships in the organization is of great importance.
      4. The supervisor has an obligation to help individuals to develop to their fullest potential.
      5. Job rotation on a planned basis helps to build versatility and to maintain interest and enthusiasm in work groups.
      6. Cross training (job rotation) provides backup skills.

7. The supervisor can help reduce tension by maintaining a sense of humor, providing guidance to employees, and by making reasonable and timely decisions. Employees respond favorably to working under reasonably predictable circumstances.
8. Change is characteristic of all managerial behavior. The supervisor must adjust to changes in procedures, new methods, technological changes, and to a number of new and sometimes challenging situations.
9. To overcome the natural tendency for people to resist change, the supervisor should become more skillful in initiating change.

C. Principles and Practices of Supervision
1. Employees should be required to answer to only one superior.
2. A supervisor can effectively direct only a limited number of employees, depending upon the complexity, variety, and proximity of the jobs involved.
3. The organizational chart presents the organization in graphic form. It reflects lines of authority and responsibility as well as interrelationships of units within the organization.
4. Distribution of work can be improved through an analysis using the "Work Distribution Chart."
5. The "Work Distribution Chart" reflects the division of work within a unit in understandable form.
6. When related tasks are given to an employee, he has a better chance of increasing his skills through training.
7. The individual who is given the responsibility for tasks must also be given the appropriate authority to insure adequate results.
8. The supervisor should delegate repetitive, routine work. Preparation of recurring reports, maintaining leave and attendance records are some examples.
9. Good discipline is essential to good task performance. Discipline is reflected in the actions of employees on the job in the absence of supervision.
10. Disciplinary action may have to be taken when the positive aspects of discipline have failed. Reprimand, warning, and suspension are examples of disciplinary action.
11. If a situation calls for a reprimand, be sure it is deserved and remember it is to be done in private.

D. Dynamic Leadership
1. A style is a personal method or manner of exerting influence.
2. Authoritarian leaders often see themselves as the source of power and authority.
3. The democratic leader often perceives the group as the source of authority and power.
4. Supervisors tend to do better when using the pattern of leadership that is most natural for them.
5. Social scientists suggest that the effective supervisor use the leadership style that best fits the problem or circumstances involved.
6. All four styles—telling, selling, consulting, joining—have their place. Using one does not preclude using the other at another time.

7. The theory X point of view assumes that the average person dislikes work, will avoid it whenever possible, and must be coerced to achieve organizational objectives.
8. The theory Y point of view assumes that the average person considers work to be a natural as play, and, when the individual is committed, he requires little supervision or direction to accomplish desired objectives.
9. The leader's basic assumptions concerning human behavior and human nature affect his actions, decisions, and other managerial practices.
10. Dissatisfaction among employees is often present, but difficult to isolate. The supervisor should seek to weaken dissatisfaction by keeping promises, being sincere and considerate, keeping employees informed, and so forth.
11. Constructive suggestions should be encouraged during the natural progress of the work.

E. Processes for Solving Problems
1. People find their daily tasks more meaningful and satisfying when they can improve them.
2. The causes of problems, or the key factors, are often hidden in the background. Ability to solve problems often involves the ability to isolate them from their backgrounds. There is some substance to the cliché that some persons "can't see the forest for the trees."
3. New procedures are often developed from old ones. Problems should be broken down into manageable parts. New ideas can be adapted from old one.
4. People think differently in problem-solving situations. Using a logical, patterned approach is often useful. One approach found to be useful includes these steps:
   a. Define the problem
   b. Establish objectives
   c. Get the facts
   d. Weigh and decide
   e. Take action
   f. Evaluate action

F. Training for Results
1. Participants respond best when they feel training is important to them.
2. The supervisor has responsibility for the training and development of those who report to him.
3. When training is delegated to others, great care must be exercised to insure the trainer has knowledge, aptitude, and interest for his work as a trainer.
4. Training (learning) of some type goes on continually. The most successful supervisor makes certain the learning contributes in a productive manner to operational goals.
5. New employees are particularly susceptible to training. Older employees facing new job situations require specific training, as well as having need for development and growth opportunities.
6. Training needs require continuous monitoring.
7. The training officer of an agency is a professional with a responsibility to assist supervisors in solving training problems.

8. Many of the self-development steps important to the supervisor's own growth are equally important to the development of peers and subordinates. Knowledge of these is important when the supervisor consults with others on development and growth opportunities.

G. Health, Safety, and Accident Prevention
1. Management-minded supervisors take appropriate measures to assist employees in maintaining health and in assuring safe practices in the work environment.
2. Effective safety training and practices help to avoid injury and accidents.
3. Safety should be a management goal. All infractions of safety which are observed should be corrected without exception.
4. Employees' safety attitude, training and instruction, provision of safe tools and equipment, supervision, and leadership are considered highly important factors which contribute to safety and which can be influenced directly by supervisors.
5. When accidents do occur, they should be investigated promptly for very important reasons, including the fact that information which is gained can be used to prevent accidents in the future.

H. Equal Employment Opportunity
1. The supervisor should endeavor to treat all employees fairly, without regard to religion, race, sex, or national origin.
2. Groups tend to reflect the attitude of the leader. Prejudice can be detected even in very subtle form. Supervisors must strive to create a feeling of mutual respect and confidence in every employee.
3. Complete utilization of all human resources is a national goal. Equitable consideration should be accorded women in the work force, minority-group members, the physically and mentally handicapped, and the older employee. The important question is: "Who can do the job?"
4. Training opportunities, recognition for performance, overtime assignments, promotional opportunities, and all other personnel actions are to be handled on an equitable basis.

I. Improving Communications
1. Communications is achieving understanding between the sender and the receiver of a message. It also means sharing information—the creation of understanding.
2. Communication is basic to all human activity. Words are means of conveying meanings; however, real meanings are in people.
3. There are very practical differences in the effectiveness of one-way, impersonal, and two-way communications. Words spoken face-to-face are better understood. Telephone conversations are effective, but lack the rapport of person-to-person exchanges. The whole person communicates.
4. Cooperation and communication in an organization go hand in hand. When there is a mutual respect between people, spelling out rules and procedures for communicating is unnecessary.
5. There are several barriers to effective communications. These include failure to listen with respect and understanding, lack of skill in feedback, and misinterpreting the meanings of words used by the speaker. It is also common

practice to listen to what we want to hear, and tune out things we do not want to hear.
6. Communication is management's chief problem. The supervisor should accept the challenge to communicate more effectively and to improve interagency and intra-agency communications.
7. The supervisor may often plan for and conduct meetings. The planning phase is critical and may determine the success or the failure of a meeting.
8. Speaking before groups usually requires extra effort. Stage fright may never disappear completely, but it can be controlled.

J. Self-Development
1. Every employee is responsible for his own self-development.
2. Toastmaster and toastmistress clubs offer opportunities to improve skills in oral communications.
3. Planning for one's own self-development is of vital importance. Supervisors know their own strengths and limitations better than anyone else.
4. Many opportunities are open to aid the supervisor in his developmental efforts, including job assignments; training opportunities, both governmental and non-governmental—to include universities and professional conferences and seminars.
5. Programmed instruction offers a means of studying at one's own rate.
6. Where difficulties may arise from a supervisor's being away from his work for training, he may participate in televised home study or correspondence courses to meet his self-development needs.

K. Teaching and Training
1. The Teaching Process
Teaching is encouraging and guiding the learning activities of students toward established goals. In most cases this process consists of five steps: preparation, presentation, summarization, evaluation, and application.

   a. Preparation
   Preparation is two-fold in nature; that of the supervisor and the employee. Preparation by the supervisor is absolutely essential to success. He must know what, when, where, how, and whom he will teach. Some of the factors that should be considered are:
   1) The objectives
   2) The materials needed
   3) The methods to be used
   4) Employee participation
   5) Employee interest
   6) Training aids
   7) Evaluation
   8) Summarization

   Employee preparation consists in preparing the employee to receive the material. Probably the most important single factor in the preparation of the employee is arousing and maintaining his interest. He must know the objectives of the training, why he is there, how the material can be used, and its importance to him.

b. Presentation
   In presentation, have a carefully designed plan and follow it. The plan should be accurate and complete, yet flexible enough to meet situations as they arise. The method of presentation will be determined by the particular situation and objectives.

c. Summary
   A summary should be made at the end of every training unit and program. In addition, there may be internal summaries depending on the nature of the material being taught. The important thing is that the trainee must always be able to understand how each part of the new material relates to the whole.

d. Application
   The supervisor must arrange work so the employee will be given a chance to apply new knowledge or skills while the material is still clear in his mind and interest is high. The trainee does not really know whether he has learned the material until he has been given a chance to apply it. If the material is not applied, it loses most of its value.

e. Evaluation
   The purpose of all training is to promote learning. To determine whether the training has been a success or failure, the supervisor must evaluate this learning.
   In the broadest sense, evaluation includes all the devices, methods, skills, and techniques used by the supervisor to keep himself and the employees informed as to their progress toward the objectives they are pursuing. The extent to which the employee has mastered the knowledge, skills, and abilities, or changed his attitudes, as determined by the program objectives, is the extent to which instruction has succeeded or failed.
   Evaluation should not be confined to the end of the lesson, day, or program but should be used continuously. We shall note later the way this relates to the rest of the teaching process.

2. Teaching Methods
A teaching method is a pattern of identifiable student and instructor activity used in presenting training material.
All supervisors are faced with the problem of deciding which method should be used at a given time.

   a. Lecture
   The lecture is direct oral presentation of material by the supervisor. The present trend is to place less emphasis on the trainer's activity and more on that of the trainee.

   b. Discussion
   Teaching by discussion or conference involves using questions and other techniques to arouse interest and focus attention upon certain areas, and by doing so creating a learning situation. This can be one of the most

valuable methods because it gives the employees an opportunity to express their ideas and pool their knowledge.

c. Demonstration
The demonstration is used to teach how something works or how to do something. It can be used to show a principle or what the results of a series of actions will be. A well-staged demonstration is particularly effective because it shows proper methods of performance in a realistic manner.

d. Performance
Performance is one of the most fundamental of all learning techniques or teaching methods. The trainee may be able to tell how a specific operation should be performed but he cannot be sure he knows how to perform the operation until he has done so.
As with all methods, there are certain advantages and disadvantages to each method.

e. Which Method to Use
Moreover, there are other methods and techniques of teaching. It is difficult to use any method without other methods entering into it. In any learning situation, a combination of methods is usually more effective than any one method alone.

Finally, evaluation must be integrated into the other aspects of the teaching-learning process.

It must be used in the motivation of the trainees; it must be used to assist in developing understanding during the training; and it must be related to employee application of the results of training.

This is distinctly the role of the supervisor.